# THE STORY OF THE BUDDHA

# THE STORY OF THE BUDDHA

BY

EDITH HOLLAND

AUTHOR OF
'THE STORY OF MOHAMMAD'

*ILLUSTRATED BY*

GILBERT JAMES &
SIDNEY W. STANLEY

GYAN

*Published by*

GYAN

Gyan Publishing House
5, Ansari Road
Daryaganj, New Delhi-110002
Phone: 011-47034999, 9811692060
E-mail: books@gyanbooks.com

*Distribution Network*
gyanbooks.com
India, USA, Canada, UK, Australia, France



ISBN : 978-81-212-4550-0 (HB)
First Published, London, 1918

2nd Impression 2020

*Printed at:* Gyan Press, Delhi.

# THE STORY OF THE BUDDHA

BY

EDITH HOLLAND

AUTHOR OF
'THE STORY OF MOHAMMED'

ILLUSTRATED BY

GILBERT JAMES & SIDNEY W. STANLEY

LONDON

GEORGE G. HARRAP & COMPANY LTD.

2 & 3 PORTSMOUTH STREET KINGSWAY W.C.

MCMXIX

**Buddha**

# Foreword

BEFORE the days of books, records of historical events were handed down by word of mouth. It was therefore but natural that, as time passed and a story came to be often repeated, many details should gradually have been added to the original narrative. Thus in all histories of very early times we find fact and legend mingled together.

So it is with the story I am about to tell you. When the narrative of the Buddha's life was told again and again, in countries far removed from the scenes where the events had taken place, tales of wonders and miracles were added to the first simple story. Many of these legends, which are very beautiful, were intended to be understood as allegories, and stories told in this way have always been favourites with Eastern people.

You will see that it is sometimes difficult to distinguish the facts from the legends which were added in later years. But, after all, why should we trouble ourselves about these things? We know that the events of chief importance in the Buddha's beautiful life are historical facts, and that is all that really matters.

# *Contents*

# *Illustrations*

# CHAPTER I: *The East and the West*

I AM going to tell you the story of the life of a very great man. He was not great as the world usually regards greatness, being neither a conqueror nor a hero in any worldly sense—in fact, for many years of his life he was a beggar. Buddha is the name by which he is generally known; but before I begin my story I must tell you something of the lands where he lived and taught—in the great mysterious East, which is so different in every way from the part of the world we live in.

The most remarkable feature of our modern Western world is Change. Think what changes have taken place in the last hundred years. Railways and motor-cars have been brought into use, wonderful inventions have been made in machinery, wonderful discoveries in science; electricity has been made use of for lighting our houses and towns, and many other purposes. If our grandfathers could see our Western world as we see it, they would hardly recognize it.

The people of the East have no wish for

such changes, and where they have not been disturbed by Western ideas their manners and customs have remained the same during hundreds of years. If one of the Patriarchs of whom we read in the Bible were to visit the scenes in which he once dwelt, he would find a familiar world, and the common things of everyday life would be much as he remembered them. He would see the oxen treading out the corn, and the women carrying their pitchers to the well as they used to do more than two thousand years ago. Even in appearance the people would be little changed, for there are no new fashions in the East, and the same graceful draperies which were worn in the days of the Patriarchs are to be seen at the present day.

The hurry and rush of our lives is also in strange contrast to the passive and dreamy life of the East. In the West most people are busy, and anxious to get through as much as they can in the day; if they are not working they are very busy amusing themselves, and few sit still to think—they would consider this a waste of time. But in the East no one hurries himself who is not obliged, and little value is attached to time or punctuality.

The West, then, is the new world of Action and Progress, the East the old world of Thought. One cannot say that either is right or either wrong. Different races of mankind possess different qualities, and try to improve the world in the direction that seems to them of the greatest importance. Thus the Greeks have taught us what true Beauty is, and left us models of beauty which have never been surpassed. The nations of the West have been foremost in science and all mechanical arts, and to them we owe most of the comforts and conveniences of everyday life. But it is to the East that we must look for the spiritual thought out of which have grown the religions which have most deeply influenced the world. It was there that all the great teachers of mankind arose—Moses, Buddha, Mohammed the Prophet of Arabia; and we must not forget that it was to an Eastern people, amid Eastern surroundings, that Christ's message was first delivered. All deep thought on spiritual matters has had its beginning in the East, and the world could better spare all the improvements of modern civilization than the wisdom of the East. It would not really matter if you had to take a pitcher to the well to fetch water, instead of turning on the hot and cold water taps; but it would matter a great deal if you had never heard of a life beyond this earthly life, and of the Kingdom of Righteousness.

The aims, then, of the East and the West have been altogether different. Who can tell which has chosen the better part?

. . . . . .

The very name of the East has a sound of enchantment and mystery, and your first visit to an Eastern country is like opening a new book of strange and beautiful fairy stories, in which everything is quite unlike the common experiences of everyday life. The gorgeous colours, glowing yet more brightly under the sapphire sky, the gay-plumaged birds, the wondrous fruits and blossoms, and the many new and strange sights make you feel as if you were living in a land of dreams.

You must not, however, picture the East as nothing but a fairyland of delight—there is sadness there, as there is everywhere, if we look beneath the surface. In civilized countries sad and horrible sights are hidden from us as much as possible, and those of us who happen to be fortunate and lead pleasant lives scarcely know of the misery that is in the world. But in the East things go their own way, and Nature's laws are enforced without interference. "The whole creation groaneth and travaileth in pain together"—we are often reminded of this by the sad sights that meet our eyes in an Eastern city. There you may see the beggars lying, like Lazarus, with their sores exposed to the scorching rays of the sun, asking alms of the passers-by; and the steps of a mosque or other large building will often be crowded with the maimed and the blind. Perhaps a man with a covering over his head may, as he passes by, reveal the face of a leper as white as snow. And in wandering through the rice-fields you may see a dying bullock surrounded by a flock of vultures, which approach as near as they dare, awaiting the coming feast.

Thus the people of the East become familiar with suffering and disease; they have more patience and resignation than we have, and are less in fear of death. The sadness of life is accepted as a thing which must be. We notice this in many ways. Music is a language which expresses the thoughts and feelings of a people. In Europe the tunes and songs which become popular are mostly of a joyful nature, but the music of the East is usually sad and pathetic, though often very beautiful. A plaintive little tune, covering a range of about three notes, will be repeated again and again in endless monotony.

But though the fact that life is, on the whole, sad lies at the root of their beliefs, Eastern people are quite capable of enjoying the pleasures that come to them. They are in many ways very simple-minded people, and enjoy simple pleasures almost like children. They live in closer touch with Nature than it is possible for us to do. Modern civilization has tended to make our lives artificial, and we spend the greater part of our time in houses, going out at stated intervals for exercise or amusement. Except the few of us who have studied the subject, we know little of the habits of birds and animals, and are apt to look on Nature as something entirely apart from man. But in the East it is different; the people have no need to study Nature in books, as their daily lives are bound up with her, and they live on familiar terms with the birds and animals. Thus in the plains of India you will see little naked boys taking the water-buffalo out to graze on the outskirts of the jungle, and the great beasts will follow the children submissively and understand their ways, though it is often not safe for the stranger from Europe to approach them.

The religions of India are very old indeed, and were practised many hundreds of years before the age of Christianity. Formerly Europeans knew very little about these ancient religions, and were inclined to consider all people professing other creeds than their own as heathens and idolaters. It is only in modern times that scholars have learnt the ancient languages, and so have been able to understand the sacred books of the Hindus, Buddhists, and others. During the nineteenth century many translations were made of these old writings, and through them we learn that God had not forgotten these people, nor left them in utter darkness. Though they never had the opportunity of coming to a full knowledge of God, enough light was given them to enable them to lead noble lives and to guide them into the paths of truth and self-denial.

# CHAPTER II: *The Kingdom of the Sakyas*

THE people of India have always been religious; their religion is very real to them, and has a great influence over their lives. The prevailing religion of India is Hinduism, or, as it is often called, Brahminism. This religion has existed, with various changes, since the earliest times of which we have any record. It seems to have had its beginnings in the worship of the powers of Nature, or rather of the beings who were supposed to control those powers. Thus there was Indra, the god of the air or sky; Rudra, the god of the storm, whose arrows, in the form of lightning, struck down men and beasts. There was a god of fire, of the sun, of the wind, and all these gods or spirits were believed to hear the prayers of men and to accept their sacrifices. In course of time new gods were imagined, or new names were given to the old gods.

By degrees the people of India awoke to the belief in a supreme God, far above these gods of Nature. They gave him the name of Brahma, and believed him to be the creator of the world and of gods and men—the source of life, in whom all beings have their beginning and their end. The Indian people have long believed in what is called the transmigration of souls, which means the rebirth of the soul in another body. Thus they think that when a man dies his soul will enter the body of some other being about to be born into the world. The good or bad actions of a man determine the conditions of his next life—if his deeds have been good, he will be born again to enjoy a happier state, but if evil, he will be born to sorrow and misery, either as a man or an animal. The Hindus believe that most of the misfortunes we suffer are punishments for sins committed in a former life. They have a great sympathy with animals, feeling that they too possess souls like their own, striving to arrive at a state of perfection. But a man must live countless lives before his soul can be perfected and fit for union with Brahma, to whom in the end all life must return, even as the moisture which rises from the sea and falls over the land as rain will find its way into the rivers and so return to the ocean. When the soul has been perfected it will no more be born into the world to suffer the miseries of mortal life, but will attain everlasting peace. It is this deliverance, this union with Brahma, which is looked forward to by all devout Hindus.

Though the people worshipped many gods, there were from very early times thoughtful men, or philosophers, who believed that all the lesser gods were but symbols of the great creator Brahma. These holy men gave up all worldly occupations and went to live in the great forests where they could be undisturbed, to think of the mysteries of life, death, and the world beyond the grave. They believed that if they subdued their bodies by fasting, their minds would become enlightened, and better able to grasp the great truths they sought to find. The people deeply respected these holy men because of their wisdom and knowledge; even kings bowed down to them, and asked their advice on important matters.

In olden days India was not under one ruler, but was divided into many small states. The rulers of these states were called rājas, or kings, but their kingdoms were sometimes very small. If you look at the map of India, you will better realize where the events I am going to tell you about took place. And first you must find the great river Ganges, for it was in the fertile lands bordering this river on either side that the hero of our story passed many years of his life, and wandered from place to place teaching his doctrines. What is now the province of Oudh was in those days the powerful kingdom of Kosala, and the province of Behar, which lies eastward of Oudh, was once the kingdom of Magadha. You will hear a good deal about these two kingdoms in the course of our story.

Across the north-east corner of Oudh flows the river Rapti; to the east of this river there is a long strip of fertile and well-watered land, where there are many rice-fields, fine forests, and groves of mango and tamarind. In the days of our story this land was an independent little state, not quite so large as Yorkshire. It was bounded on the east by the river Rohini, which flows into the Rapti near the present city of Gorakhpur; to the north rose the dark mountains of Nepal, and beyond these the snowy peaks of the Himālaya. The inhabitants of this land were known as Sakyas, and on the banks of the Rohini stood their capital —Kapilavatthu. Eastern names are always rather hard to remember, and, as this is an important one, which must not be forgotten, I will tell you the story of the founding of the city, and you will then understand the meaning of its name, as well as that of the tribe who possessed this land.

Long, long ago, so far back in the dim mist of bygone ages that it is impossible even to guess at the date, there was a certain King who had five sons. He reigned over a country called Potala. He had promised the Queen that he would make his youngest son heir to the throne, and when this boy grew up the four elder sons were banished. Accompanied by their sisters and a great number of attendants, they left their royal home, to seek their fortunes elsewhere. Turning their steps northward, they travelled many weary days, until at last they came to a rich and fertile land, where rivers flowed and thick forests grew, and in the far distance the white summits of the Himālaya stood up against the deep blue of the sky.

Near a pleasant river the brothers stayed their wanderings, built themselves huts of leaves, and provided their food by hunting the wild beasts in the neighbouring jungles. Now, on the banks of this river lived a hermit, a holy man, who had retired from the world to spend his days in pious meditation. Kapila, as the hermit was named, gave the brothers much wise advice, and in the end persuaded them to build a city. He marked out the boundaries with golden sand mixed with water, and when the building was finished the city was named Kapilavatthu. The word 'vatthu' means 'soil,' and as the hermit Kapila had given the land on which the city stood it was called the Soil of Kapila, or Kapilavatthu.

Some time after this the King of Potala, inquiring as to what had become of his four sons, was told the story of their adventure. When he heard how they had wandered into a strange land and founded a city of their own, he was filled with wonder at their boldness, and called them daring youths. And from that day the King's sons, and their descendants after them, were known as the Sakyas, which means 'the Daring,' or 'Enterprising.' Thus was founded the kingdom of the Sakyas, and the old stories relate that many hundred kings succeeded these adventurous youths, and ruled the land from Kapilavatthu. In the course of time a second city, named Koli, was built on the other side of the river Rohini.

# *The Story of the Buddha*

Between five and six hundred years before the birth of Christ King Suddhodana reigned over the Sakya land. He was a descendant of one of the four brothers whose story I have just told you. King Suddhodana married the two daughters of the King of Koli, who was related to him. The names of the King's wives were Māyā and Pajāpatī. Up to the time of which we are writing neither of them had any children, and it was a great grief to the King that he had no son to succeed him.

Now it happened that Queen Māyā had four dreams, in which there appeared many signs and wonders, and in the last of her dreams she saw a great multitude of people who bowed down to her. As dreams were considered of importance in foretelling events, the King sent for sixty-four wise men, who were invited to the palace to explain the meaning of the Queen's dreams. A feast was prepared, and rice and honey served in gold and silver dishes ; costly presents of cattle and silken robes were made to the wise men, for they were held in great honour. When they had discussed the meaning of the dreams, they told the Queen to rejoice, for she would have a son, who would have on him the thirty-two marks of a great man. But

**The Prophecy of the Wise Men**
Sidney Stanley

there was a choice between two different kinds of greatness. "If," said the wise men, "he stays in his royal home, he will become a mighty ruler, such as only appears in the world once in ten thousand years—his conquests shall extend to the far corners of the earth, and all nations shall bow down to him. But if," the wise men continued, "he chooses to renounce the world, to leave his home and go into homelessness, shaving his head and putting on the clothes of a beggar, then he will become a great saint—an enlightened one."

In due time a son was born to Queen Māyā, and great were the rejoicings in all the land of the Sakyas. The legends tell of many signs and miracles that took place at the time of the child's birth. All nature seemed to rejoice—springs of water burst forth from the dry ground, cool breezes gently stirred the trees of the forests, and a great light illumined the whole earth. The world of spirits rejoiced, and the *devas*, or angels, made offerings of flowers to the new-born babe.

On a mountain in Himālaya dwelt a holy man. Hearing of the birth of the child, he came to see him, and, taking him in his arms, prophesied that he would become a Buddha, or Enlightened One; "but," said the old man sadly, "I shall not live to see that come to pass." And King Suddhodana, hearing of the babe's future greatness, bowed himself down before him.

Seven days after the birth of her son, Queen Māyā died, but her sister Pajāpatī, the King's other wife, took care of the child as if he had been her own, and became a second mother to him. The Prince was named Siddhattha, and grew up in his father's house beloved of all.

## CHAPTER III: *The Youth of Siddhattha*

YOU will notice that the hero of our story is called by the various names of Buddha, Siddhattha, and Gotama. Siddhattha was the name given to the Prince by his parents, like our Christian names, and Gotama was his family name. It is curious that it should still be the family name of the chiefs of the Indian village which stands on the old site of Kapilavatthu. The meaning of Buddha is 'the Enlightened,' or 'Awakened,' so it is not properly a name, but a title, which was given Gotama when he had gained the highest knowledge and become a teacher of mankind. He is often called Gotama the Buddha. There were many other titles which his followers gave their master—that of Sakyamuni, 'the Wise Man of the Sakyas,' is commonly used by the Chinese Buddhists at the present day. He was also called Sakya-sinha, 'the Lion of the Sakya Tribe,' Jina, 'the Conqueror,' Bhagavat, 'the Blessed One,' and various other titles. But in speaking of the time when the Prince lived in his father's house, as the heir to his throne, we will call him Siddhattha.

King Suddhodana was devoted to his little son, who, while still in his nurse's arms, had won the affections of all who came near him by his beauty and gentle ways. But as the King looked on the child the prophecies of the wise men came to his mind, and filled him with anxiety. "If he stays in his home, he will become a great monarch, but if he goes away into homelessness, he will become a Buddha, a teacher of mankind." And the King longed to keep his son near him, and to see him crowned with earthly greatness. He determined to surround him with every luxury, that he might rest contented in his home, and gave orders that no sad or dreadful sight was ever to come before the Prince's eyes. No one deformed or ugly was allowed to come near the palace; the young Prince was tended by beautiful and attractive nurses and waited on by a large number of servants ready to attend to any wish he might express.

The Sakya land was a rich and fertile country; broad rivers, flowing down from the Himālaya range, watered the many rice-fields which covered the low-lying ground between the dense forests. Agriculture was the chief occupation of the Sakya people, and, as rice was their staple food, the rice crops were as important to them as are the wheat harvests to the nations of Europe and America. King Suddhodana himself owned many acres of cultivated land. It may interest you to know that the name 'Suddhodana' means 'pure rice.' This may sound a strange name to our ears, but it is really much the same as the English name 'Wheatcroft,' which must, in the first place, have been given to a man who possessed a wheat-field.

Every year there was a ploughing festival, which the King and all the Sakya lords attended. The city of Kapilavatthu was decked with flags and garlands of flowers, and there was a general air of holiday-making as the gaily dressed crowds made their way through the city gates to the place chosen for the festival. A thousand ploughs stood ready, and to each plough was yoked a pair of oxen. The King himself, as well as his ministers, took part in the ploughing. The King's plough was ornamented with gold, and the horns of his oxen were tipped with gold; the ministers' ploughs were ornamented with silver.

When Prince Siddhattha was still a young child he was taken to the ploughing festival.

Probably the King was so proud of his beautiful son that he wished all the people to see him, and hail him as their future king. The royal procession left the palace in great state. It is easy to imagine the gay scene—the narrow streets crowded with men, chariots, and horses, as well as elephants, and filled with all the noise and bustle of an Eastern town. Drums were beaten to announce the procession and warn the people to clear the way, as the King passed by surrounded by his ministers, his robes glistening with gold and jewels.

On arriving at the ploughing fields the King ordered the little Prince's couch to be spread in the shade of a lofty jambu-tree, a little removed from the crowd. A rich canopy was placed over the couch, which was shaded by curtains.

While the King was away for the ploughing, the Prince's nurses, hearing the shouts and cheering of the crowd, ran out to enjoy the gay scene, meaning to return immediately; but so engrossed were they, as they watched the King and his nobles guiding their gold and silver ploughs, that they forgot all about the Prince. Suddenly noticing that the sun had travelled far to the west, the nurses hurried back, expecting to find the Prince's couch exposed to the fierce rays of an Indian sun. Great was their astonishment to see the deep shadow of the jambu-tree still sheltering the Prince, while the shadows of all the other trees had moved round with the sun. Looking inside the curtains, they found the young child sitting cross-legged, as an Indian holy man sits when he is meditating.

The attendants ran and told the King of the miracle which had taken place. When King Suddhodana arrived and saw the shadow of the tree, he marvelled greatly, and bowing down before his son did homage to him.

It is very natural that stories of miracles and wonders should be woven into the histories of the lives of great men. We must remember that at the time of which we are writing (that is, between five and six hundred years before Christ) there were no written records of events. All history was transmitted by word of mouth until long after the events had taken place; and, though the Indians have wonderful memories, it is only natural that, as time passed, legends should have been mixed with the true stories. We must take the old tales as we find them, with their historical facts often shining through a halo of glory, in the same way that the setting sun appears to us, through the mists of evening, to be clothed in robes of purple and gold. The Indian people have always believed in spirits and fairies; every tree is supposed to have its guardian spirit, and probably it was thought that the spirit of the jambu-tree would have protected the little Prince when he was left alone, and so the pretty legend of the shadow came to be invented.

When Prince Siddhattha was old enough to learn his lessons he was sent to a wise old man, who taught five hundred other Sakya children. But Siddhattha surpassed them all in knowledge; in arithmetic and in all other branches of learning he seemed to know as much as his teacher. He also learnt to manage elephants, and one of his uncles taught him to shoot with a bow and arrow.

Siddhattha had a half-brother called Nanda, and a cousin called Devadatta, and probably the boys often played together in the lovely palace gardens which extended along the river-bank. Devadatta was a bad-tempered boy, and from the first showed an envious disposition. He could not bear that every one should think so much of his cousin Siddhattha, and throughout his life did everything he could to oppose him.

It happened that a large tree, standing on the banks of the Rohini, had been uprooted in a storm and had fallen across the river. The tree acted as a dam, and all the fields round Kapilavatthu were flooded, while the town of Koli, which stood some distance down stream, was very short of water. The tree was so heavy that the people could not get it out of the river, but Siddhattha, who was now a young man and renowned for his great strength, went down and removed it without any difficulty, though all the young Sakyas had tried in vain to do so. As the Prince was going through the royal gardens on his way to the river, a flock of wild geese passed overhead. Devadatta, seeing the geese, shot an arrow into their midst, and one of them fell, wounded, just in front of Siddhattha. He felt a tender compassion for the poor bird that lay bleeding at his feet; lifting it up he drew out the arrow and carefully bound up the wound. Presently a messenger, sent by Devadatta, arrived to claim the bird; but Siddhattha refused to give it up, saying that it belonged to him who had saved its life, not to him who had tried to kill it. This was the first quarrel between the cousins.

Now that Siddhattha had grown to manhood, the King decided that the time had come for his son to marry. He hoped that, by providing him with all the pleasures that this world can give, he would prevent the fulfilment of the prophecy that the Prince would leave his home and go into homelessness. Suddhodana had three beautiful palaces built for his son, suited to the three seasons, one for the heat of summer, one for the cold weather, and one for the rainy season. In India the climate is not so changeable as it is in England, and there are fixed seasons of heat, cold, and rain.

The palace built for the great heat of India had cool marble courts, open terraces, and a garden shaded by lofty trees. The winter palace was lined with wood, and hung with warm rugs and tiger skins. And the palace for the rainy season was built of bricks and lined with coloured tiles. Of these stately palaces, one was nine, one seven and the other five stories high.

Now of all the Sakya girls none was so lovely and charming as the Princess Yasodharā, Siddhattha's cousin, so she was chosen by the

King to be his son's wife. When the marriage ceremony took place Kapilavatthu was decked out as a city of the gods, and feastings and rejoicings continued for many days. Siddhattha dearly loved his beautiful bride, who was as gentle and good as she was beautiful, and the two seem to have lived happily together in the luxurious homes which the King had provided for his son.

Suddhodana must have felt more easy in his mind when he saw the Prince enjoying all the pomp and luxury with which he had surrounded him. There were forty thousand dancing girls dressed in beautiful clothes, wearing veils of many colours, and jingling bracelets and anklets. Some had sweet voices and could sing many pretty songs, others could play the lute; so whenever the Prince was weary or wanted amusement he had but to ask for a dance, a song, or a soft melody on the lute, and his wish was immediately fulfilled.

After a while it seemed to the King's brothers, and the other Sakya lords, that Siddhattha was devoting too much of his time to pleasure; it was not right, they said, that the King's son should think only of his pleasures, learning nothing of those things which a man ought to know. If war were to break out how could he lead the Sakyas to battle? So they went to the King and told him what was in their minds. When Suddhodana told his son that his relations complained that he neglected his duties, Siddhattha said that he would prove his skill in all manly exercises by competing with the bravest in the land. So a time was appointed for the sports, and the criers went forth into the city, beating drums, to announce the event.

The people gathered together in great numbers to see the Prince and the young nobles show their skill in archery, fencing, and all the arts which a Sakya should know. Some of the archers aimed so well that they could split a hair. Devadatta had always been considered the best shot with the bow and arrow, and Nanda was famous as a swordsman, but Siddhattha outshone them both. Now in a temple there hung the great bow which had belonged to Siddhattha's grandfather, Sinhahanu; this was brought out that the youths might try their strength. But none was able to string the bow except Siddhattha, and when he shot his arrow it flew so far that all the people marvelled. In every trial of strength and skill Siddhattha was the victor.

The Sakya lords had now no cause to fear that the Prince was behindhand in any manly art, and they all acknowledged that he was a worthy son of the great race of which he came.

# CHAPTER IV: *The Great Renunciation*

IN the last chapter you heard of the Prince's marriage to Yasodharā, and of the warlike games in which he overcame all his opponents, and won back the good opinion of the Sakya lords. Of Siddhattha's life during the ten years following these events we know nothing—the old stories are silent—until at the age of twenty-nine we find him still living in the midst of all the luxury with which his father had thought to bind his affections to earthly glories. For Suddhodana still fondly hoped that his son might become one of the greatest rulers the world had ever seen. "If he does not leave his home in twelve years, he will become king of the whole earth"—so had a wise man spoken, and the time was nearly passed.

We cannot doubt that during these ten years Siddhattha had thought deeply over many things. The Indians have very inquiring minds and wonderful imaginations, and the great questions of religion have always been discussed by their learned men. Perhaps the idea that he was born to help the world had already dawned on Siddhattha's mind, though he might not understand how he was to do this. From his earliest years he had shown a tender compassion toward all living beings, whether men or animals, but of real suffering and misery the Prince as yet knew nothing. So well had the King watched over his son that Siddhattha had never seen any sad or terrible sight, had never heard anything of sorrow, sickness, and death. When he drove through the city in his chariot he saw only the people who looked happy and contented, for the maimed, the sick, the blind, were commanded to remain hidden from his sight.

You will wonder why it was that Suddhodana was filled with anxiety lest his son should see anything that might distress his mind. It was because it had once been prophesied that the Prince would not leave his home until he had seen four things which would so impress him with the sadness of our mortal life that he would renounce the world. "If he does not see these things," the King argued, "he will not think of going into homelessness, and so will become the greatest monarch the world has ever seen."

At some distance from the palace were the

beautiful gardens to which Siddhattha sometimes drove in his chariot. Trees covered with sweet-scented blossoms made a pleasant shade during the noonday heat, and various kinds of lovely lotus flowers bloomed round the edge of a crystal lake, in which the Prince bathed on summer evenings. One day Siddhattha, wishing to go to the gardens, called Channa, his faithful charioteer, and told him to make ready his chariot, for he would drive through the city to the pleasure grounds. The Prince mounted his gilded chariot, drawn by four milk-white horses covered with trappings of gold. As he passed through the streets the people crowded to see him, and bowed down before him, for they all loved him for his beauty and gentle manners. And Siddhattha looked graciously at his people, and was glad to see them look so happy.

Suddenly into the middle of the road, just in front of the Prince's chariot, tottered an old man. His body was bent with age, and he leaned upon a staff, for his legs were so weak and shrunken that he could scarcely stand. The few hairs on the old man's head were white, his eyes were dim and bleared, and he stretched out a shrivelled hand, begging for alms.

Siddhattha had never seen so pitiful a sight, and was quite overcome. Turning to Channa, he said: " Why is this man so different from other men ? what thing has so changed him that even his hair is of a different colour to that of ordinary men ? or has he always been thus ? " Channa, whose answer was inspired by the angels, replied: " Prince, this is old age; this man has lived many years. All men become like him if they live long enough."

Siddhattha ordered Channa to drive back to the palace. He was in no mood to enjoy the delights of the pleasure grounds, and became silent and thoughtful. He could not forget the sight of the helpless old man, and felt as though the sun were darkened and all the beauties of earth had faded away. When he arrived at the palace Súddhodana asked the attendants why the Prince had so soon returned from his drive. When he heard that his son had seen an old man—the first of the four omens—he was filled with dismay. Hoping to distract Siddhattha's mind and make him forget his sadness the King ordered the beautiful dancing girls to perform their most graceful dances and sing their sweetest songs before the Prince; and guards were posted round the city, at the four points of the compass, with strict orders to stop the Prince if he should try to make his escape.

By degrees the vision of the old man faded somewhat from Siddhattha's mind, as the recollection of anything sad or disagreeable is apt to do as time passes. So one day he ordered his chariot, and took the way to the gardens. But he had not gone far when he saw a man lying by the roadside who seemed to be suffering great pain; his body was swollen and discoloured, and he lay groaning aloud in his agony, being too weak to raise himself from the ground. Siddhattha, moved with compassion, sprang from his chariot to see how he could help the poor man. Calling to Channa he exclaimed: "What has come to this man that he cannot stand? How is it that he has lost the use of all his powers, and why is he so distressed?" Channa replied: "This is sickness; from day to day we cannot tell if we shall be struck down by disease and be even as this man." And the Prince returned to the palace as before, for he felt that all

**Siddhattha and the Sick Man**
Sidney Stanley

pleasures were vain when such deep sadness shadowed the world.

Again, after a while, the Prince drove out in his chariot, and this time he saw some men carrying a still and lifeless form on their shoulders; women with their hair all disordered followed them, wailing aloud and weeping bitterly. Siddhattha gazed at them in awe and wonder. "What are these men doing?" he asked Channa, "and what is that still shape they are carrying?" Channa replied: "O Prince, all men will be like that still shape when life shall have passed away; that which you see is Death." And the Prince returned to the palace very sad and thoughtful; one by one the glories of earth seemed to be fading away, and happiness was but a dream—a passing vision—scarce seen before it vanished.

The King was now in despair, all his care and watchfulness had been of no avail, and Siddhattha had beheld three of the four omens which it had been prophesied he would see before renouncing the world. There remained but one more, and Suddhodana felt he was undone if he could not prevent his son seeing the last.

Fearing that Siddhattha might try to escape

during the night, the King had the guards increased at every point. He himself watched the eastern gate of the city, while his three brothers, each with a numerous guard, posted themselves at the northern, southern, and western gates. A detachment of troops under the King's nephew, Mahanāma, was stationed in the centre of the city, and patrolled the streets all night.

Yet another day the Prince drove out in his chariot attended by Channa, and when on his way to the gardens he noticed a man quite unlike anyone he had ever seen before. He wore plain clothes of a dull orange colour, and his hair and beard were shaved ; he carried a bowl in his hand, and went from house to house begging for scraps of food. Siddhattha was so struck by the beggar's peaceful and happy expression that he asked Channa about him. Channa, whose answers to the Prince's inquiries had always been inspired by the angels, replied : "The man that you see, O Prince, is a good and righteous man who has forsaken the world, and, having given up all he had, is obliged to beg his food from day to day."

Siddhattha stopped and spoke to the man,

and suddenly all his doubts and difficulties cleared away and what he ought to do became plain to him. He thought to himself, "I will do as this man has done; I will give up everything I possess and go into homelessness. So shall I find peace of mind and learn the wisdom which shall teach mankind how to overcome the miseries of mortal life." So resolved, Siddhattha drove on to the gardens, feeling a peace he had not known for many days. He spent the day enjoying the beauties of the pleasure grounds, and toward evening bathed in the lake. After this he lay resting on a large flat stone, while his attendants brought perfumes and ointments and magnificent robes of various colours. The Prince allowed himself to be adorned with great splendour, and his turban, which was wound round his head in countless folds, was fastened with glittering jewels. "This is the last time," he thought, "that I shall wear these robes of state."

Just as Siddhattha was ready to mount his chariot, a messenger arrived with the news that a son had been born to the Prince's wife, Yasodharā. Siddhattha became thoughtful, and said: "I shall find it hard to break this new tie—it is an impediment." His meaning was that the birth of his child would make it all the harder for him to leave his home and those he loved. When Suddhodana heard what his son had said on receiving the news, he called his grandson ' Rāhula,' which means ' Impediment.'

On his return to the city the Prince found all rejoicing over the glad news of the birth of a successor to the throne, for Rāhula was the King's only grandson. Hailing him with shouts of joy, the people followed the Prince's chariot, wondering the while at his glorious appearance. There was a young girl, Siddhattha's cousin, who watched the procession from her house-top, and sang a pretty verse to greet him, saying how blessed were the mother, father, and wife of so glorious a Prince. Siddhattha thought, " Blessed is he who overcomes all troubles of the mind, for such a one is the blessing of peace," and he sent the girl a pearl necklace as thanks for her pretty song.

That night the sound of music and sweet songs floated through the palace halls, and dancing girls, beautiful as heavenly beings, moved gracefully to and fro, their anklets jingling as they moved, while a hundred lamps shed a light as of fairyland upon the scene. But Siddhattha, wearied with all he had gone through, heeded none of these things, and fell asleep. The musicians and the dancers, waiting till the Prince should wake, at last fell asleep too.

At midnight Siddhattha awoke; he rose, and stepping softly to the door of the chamber called in a low voice, "Channa." Channa, who was sleeping on the threshold, answered, "My lord, here am I." "Go," said the Prince, "and saddle me a horse; to-night I will leave my home!" And Channa obeyed his master's orders. Siddhattha now felt a great longing to hold his child in his arms before he went away, and going softly to the entrance of Yasodharā's room, he looked in. By the light of a dim lamp he could see his wife sleeping on a bed of jessamine flowers, while her hand rested on the babe's head. And Siddhattha thought, "If I move her hand I shall wake her, and then she will not let me go." So he dared not touch his child, but stood and watched the two for some time, then, mastering himself with a great effort, he turned and went away.

Out into the white moonlight Siddhattha stepped—into the palace court, where Channa was waiting for him with his favourite horse Khantaka. It was the 1st of July; the moon was full, and shone with so white a light you might have thought the snows of Himālaya covered the land. It was unusually still, there was no sound but the croaking of the frogs by the river bank. The Prince sprang on to Khantaka's back, and Channa caught hold of the horse's tail and followed his master. They passed through the narrow streets of the city, by day filled with clamour and bustle, now silent and deserted. None heard the tramp of Khantaka's hoofs, for the *devas*, scattered flowers in his path so that no sound might be heard; none knew that Prince Siddhattha was riding forth from his royal home into homelessness.

As he neared the city gates a dark shadow appeared in the moonlit sky. This was Mara the Tempter, the Spirit of Evil, who sought to turn the future Buddha from his course. "Stay, my lord," he cried, "go not hence and in seven days I will give you all the kingdoms of the earth, and you shall rule over them." Siddhattha answered: "I know

**Siddhattha's Departure from Yasodharā**
Gilbert James

well that I might possess the kingdoms of the earth, but I am not seeking earthly greatness. I will strive to become a Buddha, and so gladden the heart of the whole world." Mara could not turn him from his purpose, but he followed Siddhattha closely as a shadow, watching his opportunity; for he thought, "Directly an angry passion or an evil desire shall arise in his mind, it will be easy to overcome him."

Now the gates of the city were so massive that it took many men to move them, but when Siddhattha arrived at the eastern gate he found it open, for the angels, rejoicing over the future Buddha, made his flight easy. And they sent a heavy sleep on all the men of the guard, so the Prince and Channa passed quietly out into the country.

They travelled far that night, and when the moon had set and the eastern sky gleamed golden with the light of day, they had reached the banks of the river Anomā, beyond the land of Koli. On the sandy beach the Prince stopped his horse and dismounted. Taking off his royal ornaments he gave them to Channa, and bade him return to Kapilavatthu. Though Channa begged hard that he might stay with his master and serve him, the Prince would not allow it. "You must go back," he said, "and tell my father and my family what has become of me." Siddhattha now drew his sword and himself cut off his long hair and his beard; he then exchanged clothes with a poor man who happened to pass by, as he thought his dress of fine Benares muslin not fit for a beggar.

Thus was accomplished the 'Great Renunciation'—the renouncing, or giving up, of home, kingdom, riches, wife and child.

And Channa returned to the city weeping and wailing, having left his royal master standing by the river-side in the clothes of a beggar.

# CHAPTER V: *The Search after Truth*

WE left Siddhattha, now a homeless wanderer, standing on the banks of the river Anomā, having sent Channa back to Kapilavatthu to tell the sorrowing King what had become of his son. And he, who all his life had been waited on by numerous servants, who had enjoyed the luxury of soft couches and fine raiment, and been served with the daintiest of food in dishes of gold and silver, had now no resting-place, and was forced to beg before he could even satisfy his hunger. Fearing to remain long so near the land of the Sakyas Siddhattha resolved to cross the Ganges and make his way to Rājagaha. Rājagaha was the capital of the kingdom of Magadha, which, as I have told you, was situated where now lies the province of Behar.

One of the few necessaries required by an Indian holy man, or monk, is a begging bowl, into which he can put the scraps of food given him in charity. Siddhattha made himself a bowl of leaves, and having walked to Rājagaha entered the city early one morning, passing from house to house to collect sufficient food for his needs. While he was so engaged, the King of Magadha, Bimbisāra, came out on to the terrace of his palace, and seeing the strange monk, was so struck by his noble appearance that he told some of his courtiers to follow him and see where he lodged.

When Siddhattha had collected enough food he left the city by the same gate through which he had entered, and sat down in the shadow of a rocky hill to eat his meal. He was not yet accustomed to the coarse food from the poor man's table, and could scarcely swallow it. So he reasoned with himself, saying: "Siddhattha, it is true that you have, all your life, been used to the dainty food of a king's household, yet you longed to give up your wealth and become a wandering beggar—how is it then that you are now so fanciful about your food?" and he forced himself to swallow his meal.

When King Bimbisāra heard where the strange monk was to be found, he went out, followed by many attendants, to visit him. So charmed was he by Siddhattha's manners and conversation that he offered to give him wealth, lands, and everything which could make life pleasant to him. "O King," Siddhattha replied, "I come from a rich and fertile country near the Himālaya; I belong to the Sakya tribe and am of kingly descent. But the world's treasures bring no peace, and cannot conquer sorrow. I am trying to find the path which leads to the highest wisdom." "Promise me," said the King, "that when you have found that wisdom you will come and teach it to me." And Siddhattha promised the King that he would do so.

Rājagaha lay in a cultivated valley surrounded by five hills, which formed part of a long range. Two miles to the east of the city, on the top of the hill called the Vulture's Peak, there were some caves which were often inhabited by hermits and wandering monks. Here Siddhattha stayed for some time, as the place was conveniently near the city, where food could be got, and yet it was solitary and suited to quiet meditation. For now Siddhattha, or Gotama, as he is more usually called after the beginning of his wandering life, set himself resolutely to seek the wisdom and knowledge he longed to attain. He had been brought up a Hindu, but the doctrines of the Brahmins, or Hindu priests, in which ceremonies and sacrifices play such an important part, did not satisfy him. Truth, he felt, was yet hidden from him, and, like some precious gem that lies buried in the dark earth, was not to be found but by long and patient search. To the quest of this hidden truth Gotama now applied himself with all the powers of his mind, all the courage that was in him. He was not the only one who devoted himself to the thinking out of the great mysteries of life and death; there were many among the wise men and philosophers who gave their lives to the study of these deep questions. One such teacher, named Alara, was so famed for his wisdom that Gotama followed him for a time as a disciple, but after learning all that this master could teach him he felt that he had got no further on the way to truth. He next attached himself to another holy man, named Udaka, but neither did this teacher's doctrine satisfy him.

After this Siddhattha decided to go away by himself into solitude and try whether fasting and penance would bring him the peace and clearness of mind he was seeking. The Hindus have always had great faith in fasting as a means of obtaining virtue and wisdom. Gotama left the neighbourhood of Rājagaha and travelled in a southerly direction, until he came to the great jungles of Uruvela, and here, not far from the present temple of Buddha Gaya, he settled himself for a life of solitude and meditation.

You must not imagine an Indian forest, or jungle, to be anything like our English woodlands, where we can wander along pleasant mossy paths bordered by ferns and wild flowers. The only paths in the jungle are those made by the wild beasts when they leave their lairs in search of food and push their way through the dense tangle of grass and bamboo. The path of the rhinoceros is a low, dark tunnel, just the shape of his thick, round body, but the lordly elephant opens a broad roadway as he comes along with a mighty crash, trampling down everything that stands in his way. During the noonday heat these forests are pervaded by a deep stillness, as though heavy with sleep, but when darkness suddenly falls, for there is scarcely any twilight in India, you become aware that the jungle is full of life—everywhere there is an awakening, everywhere movement, as the wild beasts begin their nightly prowls in search of food. But the holy man, who has settled himself at the foot of a tree for solitary meditation, will give no heed to the trumpeting of the wild elephants, or the roar of the tiger, for his mind is intent on the things of another world. To this day the holy men of the Hindus retire into these wild solitudes, and hundreds are every year carried off and devoured by wild beasts.

Thus did Gotama make his home in the forests of Uruvela, passing his days in meditation and awaiting the peace he longed for. After a while he fell in with five other monks, who were so struck by his great goodness and holiness that they attached themselves to him as disciples. Much did they marvel at the resolution and strength of mind which enabled Gotama to continue fasting for long periods of time. "He must be a very holy man," they said to one another; "he will assuredly become a Buddha."

I have told you that the Hindus believe in the rebirth of the soul. A 'Buddha' is a man, who, having striven for virtue and holiness through many successive lives, at length attains perfection and gains the wisdom which enables him to become a teacher of mankind. The Buddhists believe that such a teacher appears in the world from time to time to lead men into the paths of truth and righteousness. As time passes his teaching is forgotten, and mankind falls back into error and sin, until a new Buddha arises to preach the law.

The five disciples remained with Gotama, serving him as their master, and expecting every day that he would tell them he had found the perfect wisdom. But as yet Gotama saw not the truth, though he sought it by every means in his power. For six long years he continued to undergo fasts and penances, until his body was so wasted that no one seeing him would have recognized the noble Prince Siddhattha. But his fame as a saintly man spread abroad like the sound of a great bell hung in the sky, as the old stories tell us.

From time to time King Suddhodana had sent out messengers to bring him news of his son; when he heard that Siddhattha was worn almost to a shadow by fasting and penance he was greatly distressed; and Yasodharā shed bitter tears, for she still loved her husband dearly and had never ceased to grieve for him from the day when she awoke to find he had left her. She now refused to wear her jewels or to deck herself with flowers, and, that she might share in her husband's sufferings, she denied herself all luxuries, slept on a hard couch, and would eat but one meal a day.

Siddhattha's fasts and penances brought him no peace, and at the end of six years he felt that he was no nearer his goal. One day, as he was walking in the forest, deep in thought, he was so overcome by weakness that he fell to the ground and lay as one dead. When the news came to King Suddhodana that his son was dead, he would not believe it, "for," he said, "I know that he will become a Buddha before he dies."

When Gotama came to himself he began to realize that his life of penance had been a mistake, and that he was not yet on the road leading to truth and wisdom. So he took food again, and by degrees his strength returned. But the five disciples, thinking that holiness could not be attained by one who ate food like ordinary men, departed and left Gotama to continue the struggle without help or sympathy. "He will never become a Buddha now," they said, and, taking their begging bowls, they made their way to Benares.

Gotama, though sorely tried, was not discouraged. It is only the truly great who are not to be turned aside from the aim they have set themselves, even after years of failure. Weaker men will blame circumstances and say a thing is impossible and not to be done, but the truly great will remain steadfast as long as life is in them.

# CHAPTER VI: *The Day of Enlightenment*

ON the outskirts of the jungles of Uruvela there was a small village called Senani. It was a pleasant spot, situated on the banks of the river Neranjarã, in the shade of spreading sala-trees. The chief man of this village had a daughter called Sujãtã. When Sujãtã was old enough to be married, she, being a pious Hindu, prayed to the god of a certain tree, beseeching him to give her a good husband and to grant that her first child might be a son. In the course of time Sujãtã was married to a man in her own village, who owned many flocks and herds, and it so happened that her first child was a son. Full of thankfulness she remembered her vow to the god of the tree and prepared to make her offering on the day of the full moon of the month of May. Rising very early in the morning Sujãtã milked the best cows of the herd, and taking the richest of the milk boiled some fine rice in it. Having cooked and sweetened the rice-milk with the greatest care, she poured it into a priceless golden vessel, fit to hold an offering to a god.

Then Sujātā put on her finest clothes and her jewels, and, carrying the vessel on her head, went out to make her offering. As she approached the tree which was, as she believed, the dwelling of the god, she noticed the figure of a man seated beneath its shade. So glorious and yet so gracious he seemed, surrounded with a shining halo in the golden light of morn, that Sujātā took him for the god who had answered her prayers. Humbly she offered the golden vessel containing the rice-milk, and then went on her way.

Gotama, for he it was, gratefully accepted the food, of which he stood in need. Carrying the vessel to the banks of the Neranjarā, he went down into the river and bathed; then he put on his yellow beggar robes, and sat down to eat his meal. During the heat of the day Gotama wandered along the river banks under the shade of the sala-trees, his mind intent on the ideal he was still unable to reach. He had been sorely tempted to give up the struggle. Thoughts of home, of the wife he had not seen for six years, of the son he knew not except as a day-old baby, of the father who had so loved him and was now advanced in years, perhaps also of the ease and comfort of his life at home—these visions swam before his eyes, filling his mind with unrest. What was the use of continuing the struggle for this wisdom which he could not attain! Again and again had Gotama fought fiercely with temptation, with the evil thoughts suggested by the great tempter Mara. At times he felt an assurance that the light would soon dawn, and again darkness and despair would possess his mind.

Not far from the banks of the river Neranjarā stood a peepul-tree, which is a kind of wild fig. On the evening of the day on which he had received Sujātā's offering Gotama walked up to this tree with a great resolve in his mind. Seating himself cross-legged, with his back to the trunk of the tree and his face to the east, he determined that he would not stir from the spot until his mind had grasped the highest wisdom—no, not though his skin were to become parched and every drop of blood dry up in his body.

Now Mara, the spirit of evil, knew that if he could not overcome Gotama before he became a Buddha, his power would be for ever broken. So fierce were the temptations with which he assailed the Holy One that the old legends have pictured a real and visible attack. They tell us that Mara, knowing that his time was short, called on his hosts to arm themselves, and the legions of hell, aroused by Satan's war-cry, gathered together in battle array. Many leagues they spread over the earth, and as far up into the sky, until the stars were blotted out, and the darkness became solid. A sound as of thunder rent the air, and the earth shook and trembled as the powers of evil were let loose; their force was like that of a mighty whirl-wind, so that trees were uprooted, mountains split in two, and the rivers were turned backward to their sources. The angels, who had come in their thousands to help the Holy One, fled to the outer boundaries of the world, unable to stand before the army of Mara. And Gotama looked round to the right and to the left and saw that he was alone. There was no help for him but in his own steadfast mind and in the power of holiness. But so strong was this power within him that the deadly darts of Satan's warriors fell harmless as autumn leaves. Then Mara urged on the fiends to tear the future Buddha limb from limb, but their fury was unavailing, and they were unable to hurt him. When Mara saw that he had no power to do Gotama any bodily harm, he tried to shake him by all the terrors that affright the human mind. On all sides flames burst forth, and columns of fiery steam rose higher and higher until they reached to heaven; the fiends appeared in shapes hideous and horrible, such as would scare the reason of any ordinary man. But though all the powers of hell raged around him, the Holy One sat unmoved—a sight most strange and wonderful, such as had never before been seen.

When the night was spent Mara owned himself defeated. "Truly," he said, "in all the world there is no man like Siddhattha, the son of Suddhodana." And the hosts of Satan vanished away as the morning dawned, leaving Gotama alone.

In the world of spirits the angels and archangels and all the winged creatures rejoiced at the victory which had been won, and came to do honour to him who had put to flight the powers of evil—'Jina,' the Victorious One, whom Mara and his hosts had been unable to vanquish. And there fell upon the earth showers of heavenly flowers, while lilies and

**Under the Peepul-tree**
Gilbert James

lotus flowers sprang up and bloomed, even out of the dry rocks.

Gotama remained seated under the peepul-tree, and before night fell there came upon him the Peace which passeth understanding —called by the Buddhists 'Nirvana.'

. . . . . . .

Like a man who comes forth from a dark prison into the glorious light, where each object appears in clearness and certainty, so the mind of the perfectly enlightened Buddha passes into the region where all truth becomes clear, all secrets of life and death stand revealed in the light of the supreme wisdom.

To Gotama, now the Buddha, life seemed no longer full of dark mysteries and contradictions, for he perceived that the universe is governed by unchanging laws of truth and justice, that the Power which makes for Righteousness regulates all things in an orderly way. This Law—the 'Dhamma,' the Buddhists call it—is summed up in the theory of cause and effect; such a simple theory it sounds, yet it is the foundation of the Buddha's whole system. Nothing can happen by chance or accident, every event is caused by some other event which happened before it. And in the same way every event must cause some other event to follow it. We see that this is true in the world of Nature; everything that happens there is regulated by fixed and unchanging laws. These same laws the Buddha applied to the things of the mind and to moral actions. Every thought, every action, brings with it its own inevitable result. From good must come good, from evil springs evil. Thus the fruit of the actions of our present life will become the seed of the character of our future lives. For the Buddhists believe that that part of man which survives death will be reborn as a being who inherits the results of his actions—that is, his character, which he has made by his actions. For our characters are not formed only during our present lives, but are the heaped-up results of many previous lives. If we misuse our opportunities of doing good, and lead a life of sin, we shall be multiplying sorrows in countless future lives.

These things the Buddha saw with a clear mind, and he saw, too, the cause of sorrow, and the way of ending sorrow. Sorrow, he said, comes from evil, from the ignorance which hides from us the true values of life and causes us to cling to the things that vanish and pass away. For all visible things are constantly changing, decaying, renewing themselves, and again decaying. In this world there is nothing fixed, no, not for the fragment of a second. From the moment you are born, your body, your mind, and all your powers begin to grow and change, so that you cannot ever be *exactly* the same for two minutes together. The same law of change affects all plants, all animals, the very soil we tread on. Even the shape of the country we live in is every day slowly but surely changing; in some places the sea is breaking down the cliffs and gaining on the land, inch by inch; in others, the land is reclaiming the sandy flats from which the sea is retreating.

You have probably often looked at the clouds on a windy day, and imagined their shapes to be those of mountains and valleys, towers and pinnacles, or monstrous beasts. Look again, a few minutes later, and all will have changed; the pinnacles may be trees, your castle a large bird with broad wings outstretched, and the huge monster a puff of smoke. Even as you look the clouds are forming new shapes; the whole scene is changing, and in a little while this picture of your fancy will have melted and vanished away altogether. Even so, the world and all visible things are ever in a state of *making* or becoming, never can they be finished or stationary.

Christianity has told us that there can be no perfect happiness in earthly life; in the same way the Buddha taught that the perfect state can only be attained when the span of our earthly lives is ended. When a man dies, leaving a debt of unpunished sins, he will be reborn, as the Buddhists believe, to continue the working out of his salvation. He may be reborn as a spirit in heaven or hell, to receive the just reward of his deeds, and then again be born into the world to finish his course. For the Buddhists believe in heaven and hell as places of temporary bliss and suffering. It is only when a being has, after numberless lives, been purified from all sin and earthly longings that he will enjoy the everlasting peace of Nirvana.

Nirvana must be thought of more as a state of mind than a definite place; you are told " the Kingdom of Heaven is within you," and in the same way Nirvana is the attainment of perfect peace within the heart. The

Buddha and a few great saints enjoyed the peace of Nirvana while still living.

Gotama told his followers very little about this other world; he gave no descriptions of jewelled cities where the righteous would enjoy all the pleasures they longed for in their earthly lives. He only told them that in Nirvana all suffering will cease, all storms of human passions be stilled, and the fires of hatred and evil thoughts extinguished. Nirvana is often spoken of by the Buddhists as the 'other shore.' When the voyager, weary of battling with the winds and waves of the restless sea of human life, reaches at length that 'other shore,' he will pass into the immeasurable calm, the Peace which passeth understanding —everlasting because unchanging.

# CHAPTER VII: *The First Disciples*

THE peepul-tree, under which Gotama was seated when heavenly wisdom enlightened his mind, has ever since been known as the sacred Bo-tree, or Tree of Wisdom. For many hundred years it continued to flourish, and countless pilgrims have visited the spot where the great Teacher first attained a knowledge of the truth.

For Gotama saw all things as they really are; few of us can do this, as our understandings are dull, and it is only those with the greatest minds who are face to face with the deep truths of life and eternity.

It would seem that Gotama was unwilling to leave the spot where he had found rest and peace after the weariness of those six years during which he was searching for Truth. We are told that for the space of seven times seven days he lingered in the neighbourhood of the Bo-tree, meditating on the Peace of Nirvana and the way of life leading to deliverance from sin and sorrow.

But there came a doubt to the mind of the Buddha, as to whether he should teach the new doctrine to mankind. The Truth, as he saw it, seemed too simple and natural for people who had been taught to believe that charms and sacrifices and priestly ceremonies could do away with sins. For the Buddha's faith differed from that of the Hindus in this —that it taught that none of these things have power to affect a man's destiny. Sins cannot be bought off. The great natural law of cause and effect cannot be interfered with by man. And thus it followed that the Buddha regarded moral conduct as of the highest importance. Not sacrifices to Brahma or Vishnu, not money paid to the priests to appease the angry gods, not fastings and penances—none of these things mattered; but speaking the truth, restraining evil passions, showing kindness to others—these were the things that were understood by the new doctrine, the 'Dhamma.' Doing good that good might follow, that the sum of goodness might be increased through countless ages to come.

Gotama, who well understood human nature, doubted whether mankind could be brought to believe in a religion having so little show or display. For it is much easier to offer a sacrifice or to utter a charm than it is to keep a bad temper under firm control. Also, it is hard for man to realize the fleeting nature of earthly things. " How," thought the Buddha, " will one who is intent on the pleasures of this life, who is heaping up riches for himself, be persuaded that the world is but as froth, even now vanishing away; that the days of man's life are as a river running swiftly by, and that nought endures but the righteousness which leads to everlasting Peace ? "

So the Buddha reasoned within himself, uncertain whether alone to possess the knowledge he had gained, or whether to spread it abroad among men. But in the end his great love for all living beings prevailed, and he determined to preach the doctrine of salvation to mankind. " Surely," he thought, " there are *some* who will listen."

Gotama intended that his old teachers, Alara and Udaka, should be the first to hear the glad tidings, but finding that they were both dead he set out to walk to Benares in search of the five disciples who had lived with him in the jungles of Uruvela.

Taking his begging-bowl the Buddha went from village to village until he came near to the city of Benares, which lies along the banks of the river Ganges. In a beautiful forest known as the Deer Park, about three miles from the city, Gotama found his former disciples. But when they saw him approaching they said one to another: "Here comes he who forsook the only true path to holiness, who gave up fasting and penance, and eats and drinks like ordinary men; we will pay him no respect." And they treated Gotama coldly, almost rudely. But he, having now no doubts in his mind, and being fully assured that he was worthy to be a teacher of mankind, explained to them that he had become a Buddha and therefore deserved their highest respect. When the daylight was fading and the evening breeze stirred the great trees of the forest, Gotama seated himself and preached his first sermon. As the words flowed from his lips a thrill of joy ran through all Nature—the flowers gave forth their sweetest scents, rivers murmured soft music, the stars shone with unusual brightness, and there was a rushing sound in the air as the *devas* came in thousands to hear the message of salvation. And the five disciples bowed themselves before Gotama and acknowledged him to be the Holy One—the Buddha. Long did the great Teacher continue speaking through the stillness of that Indian night, 2500 years ago; and the words he uttered have ever since been treasured up in the hearts of those whom he has led into the way of Peace.

To found the Kingdom of Righteousness—that was what the Buddha said he was come to do; and then he explained the meaning of the 'Four Noble Truths,' which all his followers must know and understand. And the four truths are these:

1. The Truth that sorrow and suffering will exist as long as the world shall last.
2. The Truth of the cause of sorrow—the clinging to earthly things which pass away.
3. The Truth of deliverance from sorrow—the conquest over self and all evil passions.
4. The Truth of the path leading to deliverance from sorrow, that is to say, the way of life which must be followed by all true Buddhists. This Path, leading to deliverance from sorrow, the Buddha called the 'Noble Eightfold Path,'

because in it were set forth eight guiding principles which must be observed by all. These were:

1. A right belief.
2. High aims.
3. Kind speech.
4. Upright conduct.
5. An honest profession in life.
6. Perseverance in goodness.
7. A right use of the intellect.
8. Right meditation.

Truly he who can observe these precepts, in the way intended by the great Teacher, will lead a noble life, and give a noble example to his fellow-men.

The Buddha also called this 'Path' the 'Middle Path,' because, as he explained, it lies midway between the two extremes, of self-indulgence, and the system of fasting and penance practised by the holy men of the Hindus. For we should above all be guided by reason and common sense, and it is wrong, the Buddha taught, to indulge ourselves so that our bodies become our masters and we have no control over our appetites; while it is equally wrong to deny ourselves the necessaries of life, and so injure or weaken our bodies.

It was no easy religion which the Buddha preached to his followers, for there is nothing more difficult than to practise perfect self-control, and no one could be a true disciple of Gotama until he had learnt this hard lesson. It may surprise us to hear of the numbers who were attracted by the Buddha's preaching, but Truth has great power, and where there is true goodness and a true wish for right-doing there *must* be Truth, even if it is not exactly the same view of the Truth which we have been taught ourselves.

One of the first converts to the Buddha's doctrine was a young man named Yasa. He possessed much wealth, but gave up all he had and became a beggar like his great Teacher. You must not suppose that to be a true disciple of Gotama it was necessary to give up the world. It was quite possible to follow the Buddha's teaching and yet to continue living in the world. Indeed many of Gotama's great friends were ordinary citizens, or householders as they were called. It was the same with Christianity five hundred years later—all who kept Christ's commandments were his followers, but some were specially chosen for the higher life, and these were commanded to forsake their homes and all their possessions.

Gotama remained for some time in the Deer Park at Benares, preaching the Law to all who came to hear him—not, like the Brahmins, only to privileged people, but equally to rich and poor, old and young, men and women. When at the end of three months his disciples numbered sixty, Gotama called them together and thus addressed them: "Beloved Bhikkhus" (Bhikkhus signifies Beggars, the name commonly used by Gotama in speaking to his disciples), "we have a great duty to perform, that of working for the salvation of men and angels, and showing them the way to deliverance. Let us part company, and each take a different way, so that no two shall go in the same direction. And you shall preach the Doctrine to all men and declare the Truths which I have made known to you. I myself will go to the village of Senani, on the borders of the Uruvela jungles."

So Gotama returned to the solitudes he knew so well, and there in the jungle he met three brothers, named Kassapa, who were worshippers of the Hindu god of Fire. They were looked upon as very holy men, and at first considered themselves greatly superior to Gotama in wisdom and knowledge, but, as day after day they heard the Master speak, they were gradually persuaded of the truth of his words, and the three brothers and their numerous disciples were converted.

Gotama, like other great teachers, often spoke in parables, taking symbols from Nature to make his meaning clear. One day he was seated with some of his new disciples on a high rock, known as the Elephant Rock, which overlooked the wide valley of Rājagaha. All at once the flames of a jungle fire shot up, reddening the sky with an angry glow; the wild beasts of the jungle fled panic-stricken as the fire crept on, like a devouring monster, consuming all that lay in its path.

Gotama, who had been speaking of the subduing of evil passions, compared the fire to the inward excitement and anxiety which consume those who are intent on worldly pleasures. The fire will burn so long as there is fuel to feed it, and the fires of hatred and avarice will burn as long as we worry and distress ourselves with earthly longings. As an instance, take the man whose whole thoughts are intent on making money; he is never satisfied with what he has, but is always craving for more; never at rest, he is consumed by anxiety lest he should lose his wealth. But in those who have given up all their possessions the fires of avarice will cool down; having nothing and wanting nothing, they will enjoy perfect peace. The sermon preached by Gotama on the Elephant Rock became known as the 'Lesson on Burning'; it is found written in the old books among the collection of sermons preached by the Buddha to his disciples.

You will remember that after leaving his home the first city which Gotama entered was Rājagaha. There he had talked with Bimbisāra, the king, and had promised him that, if he ever found the wisdom he was seeking, he would return and teach it to him. Thinking now upon this promise, Gotama left the jungle of Uruvela and took the road to Rājagaha, accompanied by a great number of disciples.

One day, as King Bimbisāra was sitting in his palace, a messenger came to him, saying, "The Master is come." So the King rose, and, accompanied by many of his nobles and courtiers, went to the palm grove where the Buddha and a thousand disciples were staying.

It was nearly seven years since the noble Prince Siddhattha had walked through the city gates to beg for his food; a beggar's life was new and strange to him, and you will remember how distasteful he found the coarse food to which he was then unaccustomed. Since that time Gotama had learnt many things—the six year's penance in the Uruvela jungle had taught him what suffering and hardship meant; he had known and resisted temptation, and in the end had found the way to peace and deliverance from sorrow. And now, as the Buddha, the Enlightened One, Gotama returned to the kingdom of Magadha to fulfil his promise to the King.

Bimbisāra was a mighty monarch, yet when he came to the palm grove where the Buddha was seated in the midst of his disciples, he bowed himself reverently at his feet, thus showing that he considered the might and majesty of a Buddha far above earthly power and greatness. Then Gotama addressed the assembled multitude, explaining the meaning of the Four Noble Truths and the Eightfold

Path leading to peace and deliverance. At the end of the discourse King Bimbisāra declared himself a believer, and repeated the form of words which it is still usual to repeat on becoming a member of the Buddhist Church: "I take refuge in the Buddha; I take refuge in the Doctrine; I take refuge in the Order." The 'Order' means the brotherhood of monks, or the Church.

Before Bimbisāra left the palm grove he invited Gotama and all his disciples to come to the palace the next day for their morning meal.

The people of Rājagaha were greatly excited when they heard that the King had been converted to the new religion, and large crowds assembled to see the Teacher and his many followers as they entered the city on their way to the palace.

When the King had entertained his guests, he begged of the Buddha to accept a gift; this was a pleasant grove, called Veluvana, or 'the bamboo grove,' not far from the city gates. For the King thought the palm grove too far away, and he wished to have the Buddha near him that he might often go and visit him. So the bamboo grove was solemnly presented to the Buddha, and to the Order of Monks. A priceless golden goblet was brought, filled with water scented with fragrant flowers, and the King poured water over the Buddha's hands, saying: "May the Blessed One accept my gift."

Gotama stayed for two months in the bamboo grove, where he was joined by the sixty disciples he had sent out from Benares. About this time two noble youths, named Sāriputta and Mogallāna, were converted, and became monks. They were afterward known as the disciples of the Right and Left, which means that they were looked upon as the two chief disciples of Gotama, and were much beloved by him.

# CHAPTER VIII: *The King sends for his Son*

YOU may wonder what had been happening at Kapilavatthu during the last seven years of our story. Neither the King, nor Yasodharā, nor any of his relations had seen Gotama since the night of his flight, when he went forth into homelessness to lead the life of a beggar. You will remember the King's anxiety lest he should lose his son, but all his precautions had been in vain, and on that fateful July night the noble horse Khantaka had borne his master away in the white moonlight, far beyond the bounds of the Sakya land. There was wailing and bitter grief in the palace when the Prince's flight was discovered, and the King had no news of his son until Channa, the charioteer, returned after some days bearing the Prince's jewels. From time to time Suddhodana had sent out messengers to find out what Siddhattha was doing and where he was staying, and great was the King's grief when he heard that his son was so changed by fasting and penance that none would have recognized him.

But one day King Suddhodana was told that

his son was well, that he had become a Buddha, and was staying in a bamboo grove near Rājagaha with many followers whom he had converted to his faith. The King rejoiced greatly, and longed to see his son again. So he called one of the nobles of his court, and sent him with a thousand men to Rājagaha.

"Go to my son," he said; "tell him that the King, his father, wishes to see him, and return, bringing my son with you."

Time passed, but the messenger did not return, neither did he send the King any word of his son. After a while Suddhodana dispatched another Sakya chief, also accompanied by a thousand men, and bade him take a message to Siddhattha. Then the King waited anxiously for news; and Yasodharā, longing to hear of her husband, gazed many times from the palace roof in the direction of Rājagaha, hoping to catch a glimpse of the travellers. But there was no sign of them, neither did the King receive any message. At last he dispatched nine more nobles, each with a guard of a thousand men, but of these also nothing was heard.

Then the King thought, "*Whom* can I trust to do my bidding?" and he sent for a man named Kala Udāyin, who had always served him faithfully; he was the same age as Siddhattha, and had been his friend and playfellow. The King said to him: "None of the messengers whom I have sent to my son have returned, nor have they sent me any word. I pray you go to him and tell him I long to see him before I die; I am now advanced in years, and the end of my life cannot be far off."

Kala Udāyin promised that he would do the King's bidding, and took his leave. Having arrived at Rājagaha, he found that all the messengers who had been sent before him had been converted and become monks, so they had thought no more of the King's message.

When Kala Udāyin went to the Bamboo Grove and took his place in the assembly to listen to the Master's words, he too was converted, and resolved to devote his life to religion. But he kept the King's message in his mind, and when the month of March was come and the scent of spring was in the air, he went to Gotama and told him how much his father longed to see him.

"And now," said Udāyin, "that the spring is come and the roads are dry and the woods full of flowers, it is a good time to undertake a journey."

So Gotama resolved to go and visit his father, and he sent word to his followers to make themselves ready to accompany him, for the monks were to lead a wandering life, travelling from place to place to preach the doctrine. As Gotama and his disciples travelled on foot, the journey took them some time, and two months passed before they arrived at Kapilavatthu. The King, who had had notice of their approach, was waiting at the city gates to welcome his son. His brothers and nephews and some of the maidens of the royal family had accompanied him, and young children, carrying flowers, walked in front of the procession.

There was a shady banyan grove outside the city gates, where huts and shelters had been built for the Buddha and his disciples, for monks must not live in palaces or luxurious houses. A banyan is a kind of fig-tree which grows in India and Ceylon ; it reaches a great height, and its branches arching downward take root, thus forming new trunks ; these in their turn throw out branches which take root in the same way, so that in time a single tree will cover a large extent of ground. Thus a banyan grove, such as the one in which the Buddha and his disciples dwelt, looks like a vast cathedral, with its clusters of natural pillars and over-arching roof beneath which the fierce glare of the sun is subdued to a dim and pleasant shade.

The Sakyas had always been a proud people. Though Gotama's uncles came to welcome him, they were displeased to see one of their race a shaven monk begging for his daily food. They had determined not to bow down before their young kinsman, but seeing the King at his son's feet they felt obliged to honour the Buddha. This was the third time that King Suddhodana had bowed down before his son; the first time was when the old hermit prophesied Siddhattha's future greatness; the second, when the shadow of the jambu-tree remained fixed to shelter the young child from the burning sun, and now, when Suddhodana saw his son as a perfect Buddha, he again bowed down before him. But though he thus honoured him, the King still longed to see his son a great monarch, ruler of all the kingdoms of the earth, and he spoke to him of the delights and splendours of his early life at home. The

Buddha replied that the joys he had gained were greater than those he had given up.

Now it happened that neither Suddhodana nor his brothers had invited the Buddha and his disciples to come for their meal on the following day. So in the morning Gotama took his begging-bowl and entered his native town. How strange must it have seemed to the people that their Prince, who might one day have ruled over them, should be begging his food in the streets of his capital! The Buddha looked so calm and serene, and his face shone with so glorious a light, that the people bowed down to him as though he had been a god.

When the King heard that Prince Siddhattha was begging in the streets, he was very angry, and, gathering up his robes, strode out of the palace to find his son.

"Why do you shame your family by begging?" he exclaimed.

The Buddha replied that those of his race had always done as he did. "We come of a noble line of kings and warriors," Suddhodana replied, "and not one of our race has ever begged his food." Gotama explained that by his race he meant the prophets of old, the former Buddhas, who, having nothing of their own, had always lived by the charity of others. And then Gotama uttered the following verse:

> "Rise up and loiter not,
> Follow after a holy life!
> Who follows virtue rests in bliss,
> Both in this world and in the next."

The King's heart was softened, and taking his son's begging-bowl from him he led him to the palace, where he provided a plentiful meal for all the Buddha's disciples. Perhaps the slaves and attendants who came to wait on the beggars remembered the very different scene, seven years before, when Gotama had last entered his father's house. Resplendent in his royal robes and glittering jewels, the young Prince had driven to the palace from the gardens; and the people, rejoicing over the glad news of his son's birth, had followed the gaily painted chariot in festal procession. But even then had Siddhattha resolved in his heart to renounce all that most men hold dear in this life. That night he had left his home, not to return until he came as a homeless wanderer, begging his food from door to door.

When the monks had finished their meal,

the women of the royal household came to do reverence to the Buddha. But Yasodharā was not with them; she had remained in her own chamber, for she thought, "If my lord still cares for me he will come and seek me here." Gotama, noticing the absence of his wife, presently rose and went to the Princess's apartments, accompanied by the King and two disciples. And Yasodharā, hearing their footsteps, rose up hastily to meet her lord. That he would not be as she had last seen him—a noble Prince in the prime of manhood, glorious in his beauty and royal state—this Yasodharā well knew; yet, when she stood face to face with the shaven monk clad in coarse yellow robes, she was utterly overcome, and fell sobbing at his feet. Then she realized for the first time how far her husband had gone from her, how wide a gulf separated them. The calmness and beauty of another world shone in his face, and Yasodharā felt that the love which had once been hers alone was now to be shared by every living being.

We may wonder what were Gotama's thoughts during this meeting with his wife, but of these we know nothing. Those who have reached that 'other shore'—the Peace of Nirvana—are beyond the reach of human passions; having conquered themselves they cannot again be conquered. But that Gotama comforted his sorrowing wife we need not doubt, for in the heart of a Buddha there is an infinite compassion and tenderness, a deep understanding of human weakness and sorrow. Gotama did not stay long in his wife's presence, but soon took his leave and departed.

The proud Sakya lords had at first been displeased at seeing their kinsman a monk and a beggar, but when they heard the Buddha preach the doctrine of peace and deliverance many were convinced of the truth of his words; several of his relations, including his half-brother Nanda, became monks and gave up their royal state. King Suddhodana, however, was not among the earliest converts, but later on he too believed and, as we read, entered the paths.

Gotama had a young cousin called Ānanda, and a wise man had prophesied that he would become the Buddha's disciple and close attendant. So Ānanda's father, fearing to lose his son, did all he could to prevent a meeting between the cousins. But his precautions were vain. One day Ananda came by chance into the Buddha's presence; like many others, he at once felt the influence of the Master's great and noble nature, and when Gotama rose up to go Ānanda followed him, and none could keep him back.

You will perhaps remember Devadatta, Gotama's wicked cousin, who had been so unfriendly to him when the two were boys together; he also became a convert to the new doctrine, and joined the Brotherhood of Monks, but his conversion was not very sincere, as we shall see later on.

Among the converts at Kapilavatthu there were a great many women; some of these went to the Buddha and begged him to allow them to enter the Order as nuns; but he would not consent to this, and it was not until some years later that he allowed women to join the Order.

But Yasodharā continued to grieve for her lost husband; her love for Siddhattha blinded her to all else, and she could not face the bitter truth that henceforth he would be as a stranger to her. One day, having put on her royal robes and her jewels, Yasodharā went with her maidens to the place where Gotama came to receive his food, thus thinking to attract his eyes, for she still vainly hoped that he might return to her. In time, however, even Yasodharā found peace in the faith of the Buddha; she entered the Order and became one of the most earnest of the nuns.

About a week after the Buddha's arrival in Kapilavatthu Yasodharā sent her son to him to ask for his inheritance. Rāhula, who followed his father to the banyan grove, said to him: "My father, some day I shall be king over this land, give me my inheritance—the treasure to which I am heir." But the Buddha thought within himself, "This treasure which my son asks for is perishable and brings no happiness, I will give him instead the sevenfold treasure which I gained under the Bo-tree, and thus make him heir to a heavenly kingdom." And he told Sāriputta, one of his chief disciples, to receive Rāhula into the Order; so the child, young as he was, entered the Order to be trained as a monk.

When the King heard that his grandson was to be a monk he was greatly grieved, and he begged the Buddha to make it a rule that, in future, a son must ask leave of his father and mother before entering the Order. This Gotama agreed to do, and the rule holds good to the present day; thus, when a man takes his vows on joining the Brotherhood of Monks, he is always asked whether he has the consent of his parents.

Several of those who might have succeeded to the throne of the Sakya land had now become monks, and so renounced all claim to earthly honours. It seems strange and wonderful that the Buddha's preaching should have had the power of making so many men and women ready to give up all their luxuries and suffer poverty and hardship for the sake of the heavenly treasures of the Kingdom of Righteousness.

Gotama remained for about two months at Kapilavatthu, and then returned with his disciples to Rājagaha.

# CHAPTER IX: *The Buddha's Wanderings*

WHEN the Buddha returned to Rājagaha he took up his abode in the bamboo grove, the gift of King Bimbisāra. There were several other pleasant groves and gardens which had been presented by kings and rich merchants. You must not, however, suppose that these places were Gotama's property. No Buddhist monk is allowed to possess property of his own, and the Buddha always insisted that gifts should be made to the Order and not to himself. Once, when Pajāpatī, Gotama's aunt and foster-mother, brought him a garment of fleecy wool which she had woven herself, he begged her to give it to the Order, for by doing so, he said, she would be honouring both himself and the Brotherhood.

Of all the garden monasteries to which we have alluded none became more famous than the Jetavana, a beautiful spot near Sāvatthi, the capital of Kosala. There was a rich merchant, named Anāthapindika, who was once travelling with five hundred bullock carts laden with merchandise; coming to Rājagaha he happened to hear the Buddha preach, and was converted. It was the great wish of this merchant to make a gift of a pleasant garden to the Buddha and the Order of Monks, and no place seemed to him so well suited for this purpose as the beautiful garden of Prince Jeta, near Sāvatthi. But the Prince refused to sell his garden. The merchant then bid a higher price, but again his offer was refused. At length Anāthapindika persuaded Prince Jeta to sell him as much of the garden as he could cover with pieces of money (the square copper coins in use at that time). The money was brought in bullock carts, and the coins were laid, side by side, over the whole garden. The merchant then built dwelling-places for the Buddha and eighty elders in this pleasant retreat. There were huts or cells for sleeping in and an open pillared hall which could hold a large assembly of people. These buildings were gaily decorated, and the large hall was ornamented with figures of ducks and quails.

Anāthapindika had a rest-house built at every league of the road between Rājagaha and Sāvatthi, and, as soon as all was ready, he invited the Buddha to come and receive his gift. When news came that the Buddha and his disciples were approaching the city a great procession went out to meet them. It was headed by the merchant's son and five hundred youths holding gaily coloured flags and banners; then came the two daughters of Anāthapindika with five hundred maidens carrying pitchers of water, and after these followed the merchant's wife and five hundred women bearing dishes of food for the monks. Lastly came Anāthapindika himself, accompanied by five hundred merchants all dressed in their finest clothes. This gay company walked in front of Gotama and his disciples to the Jetavana, or Jeta Garden, where the merchant solemnly presented his gift. A golden bowl was brought, and Anāthapindika poured water over the Buddha's hands, saying, "I give the Jetavana Monastery to the Blessed Buddha and the Brotherhood of Monks, both to these now present and any who may come hereafter." It was indeed a noble gift, and the Buddha showed how much he valued it by spending many rainy seasons in the beautiful Jeta Garden.

During the fine weather the members of the Brotherhood separated, travelling in different directions to preach to the people in all the villages; but when the rains began the disciples met together and gathered round the Master in some quiet retreat.

A rainy season in India is very different from the wet weather we are accustomed to in the West. In India the seasons are more regular than they are in our variable climate, and, after a long period of uninterrupted fine weather, the rainy season, or Monsoon, sets in, and continues for about three months. When the sky has been, for many weeks, clear as polished brass and the heat dry and scorching, like the heat of a furnace, there comes at last a welcome change. There is a scent of moisture in the air, dark purple clouds gather on the horizon, gradually overspreading the sky. Frequent lightning and the distant roll of thunder announce the coming deluge, until the clouds burst over the land, and the rain, descending in torrents, continues with short intervals for weeks together. Sometimes the rains do a great deal of damage—rivers overflow their banks, whole villages being swept away by the floods, and hundreds of men and cattle drowned. But, notwithstanding the destruction that is, at times, caused by the Monsoon, it is as necessary to the well-being of the Indian people as is the rise of the Nile to the inhabitants of Egypt. Without a sufficient rainfall the crops would fail and the people die of famine. So the Monsoon is eagerly looked for as the bringer of fertility and plenty.

For the monks the rainy season was a time for quiet meditation and religious training, answering, in many respects, to our season of Lent. Some of the Buddha's most famous sermons were preached during the rains, in one or other of the garden monasteries to which it was his habit to retire.

Many people imagine that the Buddha's life was mostly spent in quiet meditation, and usually think of him as seated passively under a tree. But, as a matter of fact, few men led a more active and busy life than did Gotama from the time of his enlightenment to the day of his death. He was in his twenty-ninth year when he left his home at Kapilavatthu; after this event he passed six years searching for the Truth, so he was about thirty-five when he began his public preaching. From this time forward Gotama's life was spent in active work; during forty-five years, for he lived to be eighty, he never ceased in his endeavours to spread the faith which he believed would bring blessings to mankind. For the Buddha looked with love and compassion on all living beings, and longed that all might share in the knowledge of the great truths he had gained under the Bo-tree.

The land lying between Rājagaha and Sāvatthi, on either side of the Ganges, is known as the Buddhist Holy Land. For it was here that the Buddha journeyed to and fro during many years preaching the doctrine of peace and deliverance; indeed there were few places in this tract of country that were not hallowed by the footsteps of the great Teacher. Wherever he went he was welcomed by the people, and all who were sad and sorrowful came to him seeking advice and comfort. For though the Buddha had attained the Great Peace and passed beyond the reach of human sorrow, he had a tender compassion for the sorrows of others.

It was in the fifth year of his preaching, while Gotama was spending the rainy season in Magadha, that a messenger arrived in haste from Kapilavatthu with the news that King Suddhodana lay sick, and was likely soon to die. Gotama on hearing this news, travelled

**Gotama preaching to his Disciples**

Sidney Stanley

in all haste to his old home, where he found his father still alive. The King, now ninety-seven years of age, longed for his son's presence as he felt his end approaching. In days gone by Suddhodana had grieved because his son refused to rule over an earthly kingdom and chose, instead, to establish the 'Kingdom of Righteousness.' He would have given all he possessed to see Gotama a mighty monarch, lord of the whole earth, instead of a shaven beggar, living a life of poverty and hardship. But as time passed Suddhodana realized the noble truths contained in his son's teaching, and he too entered the pathway of Peace.

It was but a few days after Gotama's arrival in Kapilavatthu that the old King died. It is the custom of the Hindus to burn their dead, and a great pile was raised for the cremation of the King's body. When all the ceremonies had been duly performed the Buddha departed, and returned to the land of Magadha.

One day, not long after these events, the King's widow arrived in Magadha and begged to speak with the Buddha. You will remember that Pajāpatī was Gotama's aunt, who, when his mother died, had nursed him as if he had been her own child. When the Buddha had first visited Kapilavatthu, Pajāpatī, and others of the Sakya women, had begged that they might become nuns. They were ready to give up all their luxuries, to wear the yellow robes and lead the same life as the monks. But the Buddha had refused them admission to the Order. "Strive for perfection in your homes," he had said, "clothed in the white robes which women wear, and aspire not to the yellow robes and hard life of the monks. Lead pure and virtuous lives, so shall you find peace and happiness."

After the King's death, Pajāpatī and many other Sakya women, among whom was Yasodharā, resolved that they would again plead earnestly for admission to the Order. So they cut off their long hair, put on coarse yellow robes, and set out to walk to Magadha, where the Buddha was staying. They arrived weary and travel-stained, with their clothes in rags, for the way was rough and part of it lay through the jungle. But when the Queen was admitted to the Buddha's presence and repeated her request, she received the same answer as before. So she went out sorrowfully and sat herself, weeping, at the entrance of the house. There Ānanda, Gotama's cousin, found her, and asked the reason of her grief. Ānanda, being very tender-hearted, went to his cousin, by whom he was much beloved, and pleaded fervently that the Queen's prayer might be granted. The Buddha at length yielded, consenting, though unwillingly, to receive women into the Order. So, rejoicing greatly, these brave women renounced all the comforts and luxuries to which they had been accustomed, and like the monks, led simple and self-denying lives. Thus was founded the Buddhist Sisterhood. Many women, taught by the sorrows of the world that happiness is but a fleeting thing, found refuge in this community of noble women. Among those who learnt this hard lesson was Kisagotamī, a native of the town of Sāvatthi. Her story is usually called the Parable of the Mustard Seed.

In India women are married very young, and Kisagotamī was little more than a child when she had to endure the bitterest sorrow that can come to any woman. Her baby, the one joy of her life, fell sick and died. So distracted was the poor mother that she could not believe her son was really dead, and, carrying him on her hip, as Indian women always carry their babies, she went to all her friends to ask them to give her some medicine for her boy. But the people looked at her in wonder and said that medicine was of no use. So Kisagotamī wandered on from house to house, repeating her request. At last a monk who saw her pitied the poor girl, and persuaded her to seek the Buddha's advice. Kisagotamī, still carrying her dead baby, went to the Jeta Garden where the Buddha was staying, and bowing herself at his feet asked him if he could give her any medicine that would cure her child. "You must bring me some mustard seed," he answered, "but it is necessary that it should come from a house where neither parent, child, nor any relation or slave has died."

Kisagotamī, still clasping her child, started hopefully on her search for the precious mustard seed. But in one house they told her that the master was dead, in another that they had lost a child, in others that a slave or some member of the family had died, and the poor girl could find no house which had not at some time been visited by Death. Then at last she began to understand the truth which the Buddha intended her to learn—that the shadow of death is over all, that there are none in this world who can escape sorrow and loss. So Kisagotamī left her dead child in a forest and returned to the Buddha. "My Master," she said, "I have not brought the mustard seed, for the dead are many, and I can find no house where Death is not known." Then the Buddha comforted the poor mother and taught her the truth of sorrow. It is always so, he explained, men count for their happiness on their loved ones, their wealth, their flocks and herds—till suddenly, like a flood in the night, Death comes, overwhelming all. It was not the first time that Kisagotamī had lost a dearly-loved child—many times before, in her past lives, had she endured the bitter grief of separation from those who were dear to her; many times yet might she undergo the same sorrow. And Kisagotamī understood that in the Peace of Nirvana alone can Death be conquered. She begged the Buddha to let her be received into the Sisterhood, and so she entered the pathway of Peace.

"This way is straight: it leads one to the other world; it is the one road to the ocean of purity."

# CHAPTER X: *The Brotherhood of Monks*

THE Buddhist Order of Monks is the oldest religious brotherhood in the world; it was founded by the Buddha about 2500 years ago, and continues to exist at the present day. There is one great difference between the Buddhist monks and those of Christian orders. The vows taken by a Buddhist on entering the Brotherhood are not binding for life. If a man finds he is not fitted to be a monk, he may, at any time, leave his monastery and return to the world; it is, however, considered a great disgrace to be dismissed for breaking any of the rules of the Order. Many take vows for a few months or any short period, especially during the season of Lent, and in some Buddhist countries there are few men who have not been monks at some time of their lives.

The aim of the Buddhist in becoming a monk is to free his mind from earthly longings and attain that calm which is the result of seeing things as they really are and understanding their true value. The Buddha taught that none can enter the path, whose final goal is the Peace of Nirvana, until he has ceased to crave for the pleasures and excitements of the world. And this very few can do without renouncing the world and leading the homeless life.

In shaving his head and putting on the yellow robes a man cuts himself off from the world and turns the stream of his life into a new channel. Outward observances are of no value in themselves. The Buddha tells us that " It is not by dirt, by fasting, or by sleeping on the bare ground, that men become pure." Still less do these things atone for sins committed. The Hindu may think that he can escape punishment for sin by offering sacrifices to the gods, but the follower of the Buddha believes that nothing can interfere with the universal Law of cause and effect. Suffering, in some form, is the inevitable result of sin—pain must as surely follow a wrong act " as the wheel follows the foot of the ox that draws the carriage." Nothing can release a man from the penalty of sin. " Not in the sky, not in the midst of the sea, not if we enter into the clefts of the mountains, is there known a spot in the whole world, where a man might be freed from an evil deed." Punishment must overtake him, sooner or later, either in this present or in some future life or in hell. The Buddhists, however, do not believe any punishment to be eternal; and when a being has paid the just debt of his evil deeds he may still work out his salvation.

It is to this task, the working out of his salvation, that the monk applies himself when he has renounced all the comforts and pleasures of life. The ceremony of admission into the Buddhist Brotherhood is very solemn and impressive; it was instituted in early days, and has remained practically unchanged for the last two thousand years. The candidate, or man about to be received into the Order, must appear before an assembly of not less than ten monks, who judge as to whether he is a fit person to be admitted. The ceremony of ordination usually takes place in a long open hall, of which the roof is supported by pillars. At one end of the hall is seated the elder of the monks, and the others sit cross-legged on mats, in two rows down the length of the hall. Then the candidate, wearing his ordinary dress and carrying the yellow robes on his arm, walks up to the elder, and, kneeling before him, begs three times for admission to the Brotherhood. He then retires to put on the yellow robes for the first time. When the candidate returns, dressed as a monk, he kneels down and repeats the form of words known as the 'Three Refuges':

"I go for refuge to the Buddha. I go for refuge to the Doctrine. I go for refuge to the Brotherhood."

This is said three times, after which the new monk vows to observe the Ten Precepts, or Commandments, repeating each one separately.

"I take the vow not to destroy life." This is the first commandment; a good Buddhist will not hurt or kill any living creature, for the Buddha has said, "He who, seeking his own happiness, punishes or kills beings who also long for happiness, will not find happiness after death." The second commandment forbids stealing of any kind. The third enjoins purity of life. The fourth forbids lies or any false speaking—we read in the collection of scripture verses, "Let no one speak falsely to another in the hall of justice . . . let him avoid all untruth." The fifth commandment condemns the use of intoxicating drinks, which leads men into sin—"Through intoxication the stupid commit sins and make other people intoxicated."

These five precepts should be observed by all Buddhists, whether laymen or monks, the remaining five refer specially to the monks, being commands against eating food at forbidden times, going to plays and entertainments, wearing ornaments, sleeping on soft beds, and receiving gold and silver, which no monk is allowed to possess.

After the repetition of the Ten Precepts, the ceremony of ordination ends, and the new monk is a novice, or beginner. He cannot be a fully ordained monk until he is over twenty years of age.

The novice, on entering his new life, becomes the pupil of an older monk, who acts toward him like a father toward his son. And the novice, on his side, attends on the daily wants of his spiritual father. It is his duty to rise before daybreak, and, when he has washed himself, to clean the house and sweep round the bo-tree, which is planted near every monastery in remembrance of the sacred Bo-tree under which Gotama obtained enlightenment. When these duties have been performed, and the drinking water for the day has been fetched and filtered, the novice sits down to meditate. By meditation we mean fixing the mind steadily on a given subject, banishing all other thoughts. Meditation on some sacred subject is the form of prayer that is practised in the religion of the Buddha.

Buddhist monks are allowed only one meal in the day, and this must be taken between sunrise and noon. So, while it is yet early, the novice follows his superior to the village for the daily round of begging. Silently the monks stand with their alms-bowls at the doors of the houses, for they may not ask for anything; silently they go on their way, uttering no complaint against those who give them nothing. The people in Buddhist countries love and honour the monks and consider it a privilege to supply them with food—even the very poorest put by a small portion of rice or a little fruit in readiness for the monks' daily visit. But only food or the actual necessaries of life may be given, for no monk is allowed to possess money. In fact, his possessions are limited to eight articles which are considered necessaries. These are the following: an alms-bowl, a razor, a needle, a water-strainer, three robes and a girdle. The three robes are the yellow beggar robes often mentioned before. They consist of three pieces of coarse cotton cloth, dyed a dull orange colour; two of these pieces are used as undergarments, the third is worn something like a Roman toga, with one end thrown over the left shoulder, leaving the right arm free.

Buddhist monks lead very simple and self-denying lives, but they do not, like the holy men of the Hindus, undergo severe fasts and penances. For the Buddha forbade his followers to practise these, having himself proved their uselessness. A monk passes his time studying the sacred books, copying them out, learning portions by heart, and meditating on the great truths contained in them; in teaching the young, for schools are attached to many of the monasteries, and in the discharge of his simple daily duties. Of ceremony or ritual there is little to be attended to—flowers are offered at the shrine, where the image of the Buddha is seated in an attitude of calm contemplation, a symbol of the Great Peace which is the goal of all true Buddhists. You must not suppose that the Buddhists worship these images. They reverence the Buddha as the perfection of manhood, the

Great Teacher, who learnt the Truth and taught it to mankind, but they do not regard him as in any way more than human. To the shrines of the Buddha, which are usually built in the shade of large trees, men and women bring their offerings of flowers. Silently they sit and meditate on the beautiful and holy life of him who showed them the way to Peace. Sometimes the monks read portions of the sacred books to the assembled people, but, in those countries where the simple faith of the Buddha prevails, there are no regular services like those of Christian churches.

Twice in the month, at the new and full moon, all the monks of a district meet together for Confession. The elder of the brethren, after reading a portion of the Scriptures, asks the assembled monks if they have any sins to confess. If all are silent the question is put a second and a third time; and the monk who, having a sin on his conscience, does not confess it on the third repetition of the question, is guilty of telling an intentional lie.

You have already heard of the Buddhist Sisterhood, which was founded by Pajāpatī, the Buddha's aunt and foster-mother. The sisters, or nuns, live together in communities, and are under the same rules as the monks. They are taught to look up to the monks as their superiors; and are instructed by them, and confess their sins to them. The sisters, like the monks, are always free to return to the world if they wish to do so, and you must not imagine them in any way like cloistered nuns. In the early days of Buddhism the Sisterhood flourished in many towns and villages; some of the sisters became teachers of the Doctrine, and even preached to the people, for Indian women of that time enjoyed much more freedom than is allowed to the Hindu woman of the present day.

Though the monks lived mostly among men, wandering from place to place to preach the truths which the Buddha had taught them, yet there were many who lived in the great forests as hermits. Indeed, a solitary life was often adopted for a time as the best means of attaining that indifference to worldly things, which is the first lesson to be learnt by the brethren of the yellow robe.

Living in the great solitudes of the Indian jungle, these lonely monks were in close touch with Nature, and learned to love and understand her as the dwellers of a busy town can never do. With no shelter but a large tree or a mountain cave, they roamed through the jungle, free and fearless as the elephant or the rhinoceros, for he who has conquered himself knows no fear. In forest glade, or wind-swept mountain height, these wanderers found freedom and joy; how deep was their love of Nature we learn from the poems, or psalms, which many of them have left us. The blossoms on the margin of the stream, the pale grey cranes rising at evening from the marshes and sailing on broad wings into the glow of sunset, the cool winds that stir the trees at sundown, the white moonbeams lighting the dim pathways of the jungle—such things as these filled the lonely watchers with a quiet joy. "They move about in peace on mountains and in forests; they are happy in finding happiness, and leave sorrow behind. . . ." Nor was it only in the softer moods of Nature that these hermits delighted, for they tell of the joy that thrilled them when the storm-clouds swept across the sky, when the lightning flashed and "the thunder-clouds in heaven beat the drum."

Thus, face to face with Nature, the monk learns his lesson—learns so to school his mind that, "like a rock it remains without being moved, in the midst of passions without passion, in the midst of anger without anger." Then is his task accomplished—"What was to be done, has been done"—cool as the snowy peaks of Himālaya is his mind who has extinguished the fires of earthly passions.

The monks are held in great reverence by the people of Buddhist countries on account of their pure, unworldly lives. Every gift bestowed on these holy men is thought to benefit the giver and bring him nearer to an understanding of the Buddha's doctrines. Though all Buddhists do not see the truth clearly enough to let go their hold on worldly pleasures, yet they regard the life of a monk as the highest state. For in a world where nothing is fixed, where change is ever at work, transforming and destroying—what is there for man to cling to but that which alone is changeless—the Peace of Nirvana. But the Buddha's teaching is hard to realise, and it is only after living many lives and enduring many sorrows, that man perceives the fleeting nature of all that he strives to attain. "Day and night this life is passing away; what subject of rejoicing is there in so brief a thing?"

# CHAPTER XI: *Some Stories of Olden Days*

THE monks, about whom I told you in the last chapter, have always been zealous missionaries, and by their efforts the Faith has spread to countries far removed from the land of its birth. For Buddhism, like Christianity and Mohammedanism, is a missionary religion, and from its earliest days has sent forth teachers to convert others to the Faith, and invite all the world to share in its blessings. You will remember how the Buddha sent out his first sixty disciples, bidding them go in different directions to announce the message of salvation. They were to preach alike to rich and poor, men and women, to the wise and the unlearned.

When the Buddha taught the simple village people, who crowded to the Jeta Garden to hear him, he often made use of parables and allegories. On many a lovely night, when the garden slept in the white moonlight, and the fire-flies glimmered in the dark spaces beneath the trees like the dim lamps of some cathedral aisle, Gotama sat in the great hall, above the circle of attentive listeners, telling them simple stories, such as they could understand, teaching them that every man must reap the results of his own actions, good for good and evil for evil. Many of the stories with which the Buddha delighted his hearers have become favourites in every European country. For the tales which we call *Æsop's Fables* came originally from India, and some of them were first told by Gotama in the famous Jetavana, or Jeta Garden. Thus, the fable of the Talkative Tortoise, of the Ass in the Lion's Skin, and many others, were well known to the people of India more than two thousand years ago. You will notice that these stories all have a moral, that is, a lesson to be learned —it is usually the wise and virtuous who flourish, while he who acts wrongfully or foolishly suffers in consequence.

Some of these Indian parables shew us how a being may, in the course of countless lives, rise, step by step, from the lowest stages to the highest—even to the summit of perfection as shewn forth in a Buddha. For the fate of every being depends on his own efforts—for good or for evil he himself weaves the thread which links his many lives together. Each life is the direct outcome of the one preceding it, so that in reality these many lives are one, and death but a momentary interruption—a change to a new phase of being.

Many of the old stories tell of the supposed former lives of Gotama the Buddha, both in human and animal form, as, for instance, that of a hare, a quail, a stag, and so on. The name by which he is called in these tales of long ago is 'Bodisat.' This means one who is striving to reach the perfection of Buddhahood, but has not yet attained enlightenment. In each life some act of virtue is performed, and a step gained on the upward path.

In a story called "The Devoted Deer," a noble stag, the leader of the herd, is supposed to be the future Buddha. There was a herd of a thousand deer living in a beautiful and sheltered valley. The king of this herd was a magnificent stag, who took good care of the deer and kept his wits well about him if any danger threatened them. One day a hunter, who was stalking some game on the neighbouring hills, noticed the beautiful stag and his herd of many deer. So he went to the King and told him about them. The King, pleased with the prospect of a good day's sport, came to the valley with all his soldiers, who surrounded the herd of deer.

The brave stag was determined to do his utmost to save the herd, he could see, however, no way of escape except by crossing a swift stream which flowed through the bottom of the valley. But the deer, especially the younger and the weaker ones, could never have crossed the foaming torrent in safety. What was to be done? The stag, forgetful of self and thinking only of the welfare of the herd, jumped into the middle of the stream, calling on the deer to spring on to his back, and so on to the farther bank. One by one the deer jumped on to the stag's back, as on to a stepping stone, and in this way crossed the stream in safety. But the stag was sorely wounded, the flesh of his back being torn to the very bone through being struck by so many hoofs. He felt that death was near, when he saw a young fawn who had not been able to keep up with the herd. He called to the fawn to hurry down to the stream, and succeeded in getting it safely over before he lay down and died.

Thus by his noble act of self-sacrifice had the stag saved his whole herd from destruction. In giving his life to save others he had performed an act of virtue, and so gained a step on the upward path leading to perfection.

Sometimes the future Buddha is represented as coming to life as a merchant, a king's treasurer, a seller of brass ware, and so forth. There is a story called "Holding to the Truth," which is intended as a warning to those who are too easily led and inclined to follow the advice of the first person they may meet.

The story is told as follows[1]: Once upon a time the Bodisat was born into a merchant's family living in Benares. When he grew up he went about selling merchandise with five hundred bullock carts, sometimes travelling east, sometimes west. There was another merchant's son, in the same city, who was stupid and dull, and wanting in resource. Now both these young merchants had collected much valuable merchandise, and each had loaded his goods on five hundred bullock carts. Then the Bodisat thought, "If we both travel together, there will not be room enough for so many carts, we shall not be able to get enough wood and water, nor enough grass for the bullocks." So he said to the foolish young merchant, "We cannot travel together; will you choose

[1] From Rhys Davids' *Buddhist Birth Stories.*

whether you start first, or come after me?" And the foolish young merchant chose to go first, thinking he would thus have the advantage—there would be more grass for the oxen, the water would be undisturbed, and he would come first into the market to sell his goods. So he yoked his oxen to the five hundred carts and started on his journey. The way to the city to which the caravan was bound lay through a great waterless desert, haunted by demons. Before entering this desert the merchant told his men to fill some large water-pots with water, and load these on the carts. When they were about half-way across the great desert they met a man seated in a beautiful carriage, drawn by milk-white bulls; ten or twelve attendants followed him, and all wore garlands of water-lilies and carried bunches of red and white lotus flowers in their hands. The hair and clothes of these men appeared to be dripping with water, and the wheels of the carriage were covered with mud. The foolish merchant greeted the traveller, and asked him if it had been raining the way he had come? "Raining," exclaimed the chief of the demons, for he it was, "it is always raining! Beyond that green forest that you will soon see, the country is full of water, the streams are always running, and there are pools covered with lotus flowers." The merchant, foolishly believing this story, was persuaded to throw away his water-pots, in order to lighten his carts, it being useless to carry water to a country where it was always raining. Then the demons passed out of sight and returned to their home.

But the poor travellers soon discovered what a grievous mistake had been made, for before them lay a parched wilderness with no sign of water. When night fell they encamped by the way side, but they had not a drop of water, so they could neither cook their rice nor give the tired oxen anything to drink. Weary and dispirited the men fell asleep, and none kept watch over the camp during the night. Toward dawn the demons came up from the demon city and fell on the camp, slaying both men and oxen, and when they had devoured them all, leaving only their bones, they went away. So all those men came to destruction on account of the merchant's foolishness in believing the demon's tale.

Now a month and a half later the Bodisat started with his caravan for the same city to which the foolish young merchant had been going. When the Bodisat and his men were come about midway across the desert, they met the demon in his carriage drawn by the white bulls. As on the former occasion he and his attendants had all the appearance of having been drenched with rain; they carried lotus flowers, and wore wreaths of water-lilies. The demon told the Bodisat exactly the same story as he had told the foolish young merchant. But the Bodisat, who had his wits about him, thought, "This fellow seems bold in his manner, and I notice that he throws no shadow like an ordinary man; he is, no doubt, a demon, and probably it is a lying tale which he tells. I will give no heed to him." So when the demon advised throwing away the water to lighten the carts, the Bodisat told him that he could manage his own affairs. And the demons, as before, passed out of sight, and returned to the demon city.

Then the Bodisat addressed his men, and told them he felt sure the stranger was a demon, and his story, besides, was against all common sense; if they were near such a rainy country as that described by the demon, would they not see rain-clouds, or hear thunder? For thunder can be heard at a distance of several leagues, and the moisture of the clouds can be scented a great way off; but no one had seen a cloud in the sky or noticed any sign of rainy weather. Then the caravan moved on again, and presently came to the spot where the foolish young merchant had camped; the five hundred carts stood full of merchandise, just as they had been loaded, and the bones of the men and oxen were scattered in all directions.

Before night-fall the Bodisat's men had made their camp; the waggons were ranged in a circle to make a strong defence, and the oxen, which had been watered and fed, were placed in the middle. The Bodisat and the chief men of the caravan stood on guard all night, with drawn swords in their hands, and the demons dared not attack them. When morning came the oxen were yoked to the waggons and the caravan started on its way. The end of the journey being safely reached, the Bodisat sold his merchandise at a high price, and he and all his men returned in safety to Benares. So ends the story of "Holding to the Truth"—of holding fast to what you know to be the right course, instead of listening to any stray advice.

Many of these quaint old stories teach us what a high value was set on acts of self-sacrifice. There is a story about a wise hare, who is supposed to be the future Buddha living one of his many lives in the dim ages of the past. The hare, we are told, lived on a mountain side, in company with several other animals. One day a holy man passed that way, and the animals were all anxious to make him some gift. Each of the others gave according to what he had, but the hare thought, "What have I to give? the only gift I can make to this holy man is myself!" Now there was a fire kindled close by, and the hare jumped into it, and roasted himself to make a meal for the hermit, thus gaining great merit, for what higher act of self-sacrifice can there be than to lay down one's life?

Another time the Bodisat, or future Buddha, is represented as a hermit living in a great forest. It was a time of famine—no rain had fallen for months, all the crops had failed, and there was not a blade of grass to be seen; the earth was so dry that it was rent asunder in deep cracks and chasms. One day, as the hermit sat under a tree in the shimmering heat, wrapped in meditation, he spied a lean, gaunt tigress with her two cubs. The beast was so wasted with famine that she could hardly crawl, and the little cubs were whimpering for the food she could not give them.

The hermit felt a deep compassion for the poor mother and her starving young, and he thought to himself, "I will perform the highest act of self-sacrifice—I will give my life for this hungry tigress, that she may feed her young and relieve their pain." And he lay down, in the path of the wild beast, who, seeing her prey, sprang on the hermit and devoured him. These tales may sound strange and unreal in Western ears, but they are full of meaning to those people of the East who hold that the highest ideal that can be reached is the entire giving up of Self.

There is a story called "The Old Woman's Black Bull,"[1] which you may like to hear. Once, long ago, the Bodisat returned to life as a bull. While still a young calf he was given to an old woman by a man who owed her some money for his lodgings. The old woman soon grew very fond of the little black calf; she fed him on rice and gruel and made a great pet of him. His name was 'Blackie,' and he was

[1] From Rhys Davids' *Buddhist Birth Stories.*

everywhere known as the 'Old Woman's Blackie.' He roamed about just as he pleased and made friends with the village children, who used to ride on his back and catch hold of his horns and tail; but 'Blackie' was so good-tempered that he never harmed them. As he grew up he became a very strong and handsome young bull, with a coat that shone like the raven's wing. One day the thought came to him, "My mother" (for so he thought of the old woman) "seems very poor; she has always been kind to me, and treated me like a son; how would it be if I did some work that would bring her in a little money?" So 'Blackie' began to look out for a job.

Now one evening the old woman was sitting alone in her house, when 'Blackie' came in, looking quite exhausted, with a bag tied round his neck. Inside the bag the old woman found a thousand pieces of money. On inquiry she was told that a caravan with five hundred bullock carts had been trying to cross the ford, but the mud was so deep that the bullocks were unable to move the waggons. The owner of the caravan, looking about to see if he could hire a strong bullock, noticed 'Blackie' grazing near the ford. He asked some herdsmen who was the owner of the young bull; he would be willing, he said, to pay a reward for having his wagons pulled across the ford, and he offered two pence for each of the five hundred carts, a thousand pieces in all. 'Blackie,' hearing this, allowed himself to be caught and yoked to one of the carts. Putting forth all his strength, he made a mighty effort, and dragged the cart across the ford. Then he was yoked to the second cart and then to the third, and so on, until he had brought all the five hundred carts safely across the ford.

When the old woman heard what 'Blackie' had done, she called him her darling and gave him some good food and drink. Then she bathed him in warm water, and rubbed him all over with oil. 'Blackie' lived happily with the old woman until the end of his days, and then he passed away 'according to his deeds,' which means that according to his deeds would be the conditions of his future life. The story of 'Blackie' ends with the following verse:

> Whene'er the load be heavy,
> Where'er the ruts be deep,
> Let them yoke 'Blackie' then,
> And he will drag the load!

Once upon a time the Bodisat was born as an Elephant in the country of the Himālaya. He was a beautiful beast, white all over, and was lord of a herd of eighty thousand elephants. His mother was blind, so, like a dutiful son, he ranged far and wide to get her the sweetest fruits, which he sent her by some of the other elephants. After a time he discovered that she got none of the sweet fruits he toiled to get for her, for the greedy elephants had eaten these themselves. So he determined to leave the herd and take his mother to a quiet spot where he could look after her. In the middle of the night they stole away and went to a cave in the mountains, close to a beautiful lake. Here the Elephant looked after his mother and brought her all she wanted.

One day when the Elephant was out to get food he heard a sound of lamentation, and came on a forester who seemed in great distress. On being asked what ailed him, the man replied that he had lost his way and had been wandering about for seven days trying to find the path. "You have no cause to fear me," said the Elephant, "I will show you the way to the paths of men." And he let the man get on his back and carried him safely out of the jungle. The forester, having been shown the right track, found his way back to Benares, where his home was.

Now at that time the King's state elephant died, and no other could be found fit to carry the King in royal processions. So a crier was sent through all the city of Benares, beating a drum, and calling out: "If any man has seen an elephant fit to carry the King, let him come to the palace to announce it." Then the ungrateful forester remembered the white Elephant who had saved his life and carried him out of the jungle. And he went to the palace and stood before the King. "O King," he said, "far away on a mountain in the Himālaya country there is a magnificent elephant, snow white, and fit to carry your Majesty." So the King sent out his elephant-tamers, and the forester showed them the way to the cave in the mountains. They found the white Elephant feeding in the lake among the lotus lilies. And he, knowing that those men had come to capture him, said to himself, "Though my strength is such that I could scatter a thousand elephants, yet I must not give way to anger, not even if I should be pierced through with knives." So he stood quietly and allowed himself to be caught and taken to Benares, a seven days' journey.

The King was delighted with the beautiful white Elephant, and had him put into a stable adorned with bright coloured hangings and decked with garlands of flowers. But no food would the Elephant eat, for he was thinking of his poor blind mother, far away in the mountains. Then the King asked the Elephant why he would not eat. "O King," he replied, "my mother, blind and wretched, is pining for her son; far away in the mountains she stands, beating her foot on some tree root." Then the King was touched by the Elephant's kindness to his mother. "Let the mighty Elephant go free," he said, "let him return to his old haunts that he may find the mother who pines for him." So the Elephant returned to his home in the mountains, and his mother rejoiced to have her son with her once more.

Another story tells that the Bodisat was once born into a rich Brahmin family. When his parents died he inherited great wealth, but he gave it all away in charity and went to the Himālaya mountains to lead the life of a hermit. Now at that time Brahmadatta was reigning in Benares. One night the King, lying on his royal bed, was startled by hearing several strange sounds. First he heard a crane screaming in the palace garden. Then a solitary crow cawed from the gateway of the elephant house. Shortly after, the buzzing of a large insect disturbed the King, then the note of a cuckoo. A tame deer and a monkey who lived in the palace also made terrified noises. The King was much alarmed by these strange sounds at midnight, and the next day he consulted the wise men, asking them if they could account for the disturbance. "O King," they said, "you are in great danger; it would be well to offer a sacrifice to turn away the anger of the gods." So the priests collected many animals and made preparations for a great sacrifice.

It happened that the Bodisat, having travelled down from the Himālaya, was staying at this time in a garden in Benares. Now a pupil of one of the wise men, having pity on the animals who were about to be slain, went to the Bodisat and asked him if he could account for the sounds which had alarmed the King. "The sounds were quite natural," replied the Bodisat, "there was nothing to be feared from them." The pupil begged him to come to the palace and give this explanation to the King; but he answered: "How can I, who am a stranger here, pretend to greater wisdom than these priests?" The pupil, however, told the King what the hermit had said, and Brahmadatta went himself to the garden to question him.

"O King!" said the Bodisat, "there was nothing unusual about the noises you heard—they were quite natural and betokened no danger to your Majesty. The crane called out because he was hungry, for the tanks were empty and he could find no food. The crow had built her nest over the gateway of the elephant house, and had laid her eggs and hatched out her brood; but every time the elephant-keeper rode through the gate he struck at the crow with his iron hook, and destroyed her nestlings. So the crow was mourning the loss of her young." When the King heard this he sent for the elephant-keeper and dismissed him.

"The caged cuckoo," continued the Bodisat, "was pining for her life in the forest. I beg of you, great King, to set her free!" And the King had the cuckoo set free.

"The stag," the Bodisat went on, "had

once been lord of the herd, and he was dreaming of his wandering life in the plains, and of the hinds who used to follow his lead." In this way the hermit made it clear that all those strange noises had been due to natural causes, and he assured the King that there was no need to fear any danger to himself. So Brahmadatta, persuaded of the truth of the Bodisat's words, let it be proclaimed by beat of drum that there would be no sacrifice, and he gave orders for the release of all the animals that had been set apart for slaughter.

Thus the Bodisat extended his love toward all creatures and persuaded men to deeds of compassion and mercy. There are many more of these old stories which you may like to read for yourselves some day. They teach that of all virtues the highest is self-sacrifice; he who forgets Self will reach the end of his voyagings down the troubled river of Life, and enter that calm ocean where no winds blow—the ocean of eternal Peace.

# CHAPTER XII: *The Kinship of All Life*

THE Buddha's message, like that of Christianity, was for all mankind, without distinction. None was excluded, and members of all the Hindu castes were received into the Order. Thus at one time we hear of a queen (the wife of King Bimbisāra) becoming a nun, at another it is a rope-dancer who exchanges her gay clothes and tinkling bells for the yellow robes of the Buddhist Sisterhood. Among the monks were some who had been royal princes, while one, renowned for his piety and learning, had been the King's barber at Kapilavatthu.

The Brahmins believe a man born in the Brahmin caste to be superior to other men; but the Buddha held that no man could be born to merit, which must depend on his own efforts alone. In fact, the name Brahmin, or Brāhmana, was used by the Buddha to denote one who treads the higher paths of virtue and wisdom. "A man does not become a Brāhmana by his plaited hair, by his family, or by birth; in whom there is truth and righteousness, he is blessed, he is a Brāhmana." And again the Buddha says, "Him I call indeed a Brāhmana whose knowledge is deep, who possesses wisdom, who knows the right way and the wrong, and has attained the highest end."

There is a story[1] about a proud young Brahmin who came to visit the Buddha, which teaches a lesson in courtesy and good manners. The Blessed One was staying in a grove near Sāvatthī. One day some of the disciples were walking up and down in the open park near the wood, when a learned young Brahmin arrived, saying he was come to call on the Teacher of whom he had heard so much. "Where shall I find the venerable Gotama?" he asked. "There is his dwelling," replied one of the disciples; "go quietly into the porch, give a slight cough, and knock on the cross-bar; the Blessed One will open the door." The young Brahmin did as he was bid, and was admitted into the Buddha's dwelling. It was the custom of the times to show respect to elders by standing while they remained standing, sitting when they were seated, or reclining if they reclined. But the young Brahmin, disregarding all the rules of

[1] Translated in Rhys Davids' *Dialogues of the Buddha.*

politeness, bore himself haughtily in the Buddha's presence, and boasted of his high descent.

"Is that the way you speak with your elders?" said the Buddha reprovingly.

"Certainly not," replied the young man. "I know how to behave when I am conversing with a Brahmin, but when I am speaking with beggars, inferior monks, or black fellows, I address them as I do you."

"But are you not wanting something?" asked the Buddha; "think rather of the object of your visit. This young Brahmin is ill-bred," he added, "but it is not so much his own fault as that of his teacher, who should have taught him good manners."

The young Brahmin resented being thought rude, and gave way to his anger by calling the Sakyas rough-mannered folk and quick at taking offence. "There are four degrees of men," he continued, "the Brahmins, the nobles, the traders, and the workpeople; of these, the three last are but attendants of the Brahmins."

The Buddha rebuked the young man for his pride by proving to him that the Sakyas had as much right as himself to boast of their descent. "But those who walk in the highest path of wisdom and righteousness," continued the Buddha, "are not concerned with such questions as birth, or the pride which compares one man's position with that of another." As he discoursed on the beauty of the perfect life, the young Brahmin, who had been so full of arrogance and self-importance, confessed that the Teacher was indeed a Buddha—one of those great ones who come but rarely to bring salvation to mankind.

Wonderful it was that so many should have chosen to follow the Buddha along the rough path of duty and self-sacrifice, when so little was said of future reward and no wonders were worked to convince the wavering. Indeed, when the Buddha heard that one of his disciples had performed a miracle, he expressly forbade the use of any wonder-working powers, for it was not thus that the Doctrine should be preached. But though miracles have no place in the Buddha's teaching, it was but natural that his followers should surround the doings of their beloved Master with a halo of more than earthly glory. And thus it was that many beautiful legends grew in time to be a part of their belief. One of these describes the Buddha's ascent to heaven to preach the Doctrine to his mother, who had died seven days after his birth. During three months the disciples could not find their Master—far and wide they sought him, but no one could tell them whither he was gone. And the legend relates that Gotama ascended to the abode of happy spirits to tell his mother, who had left this earth before he began his ministry, that he had found the Truth. The Buddhists imagine heaven to be a place where the righteous are reborn to enjoy an age of bliss—but an age which has an ending, for the glories of heaven, like those of earth, must fade and pass away, and nought but the Peace of Nirvana shall remain. With all the beauty and vividness of Eastern imagination, the disciples pictured their Master in the abode of blessed spirits. Seated on a shining throne in the midst of a celestial grove, he taught his mother the everlasting Truths of the Doctrine, while myriads of listening angels and spirits rejoiced to hear the message of salvation. When the Buddha descended to earth he trod upon a jewelled stairway, glistening, like the rainbow, with hues of precious gems.

The disciples were rejoiced when they had their Master with them once more, and they followed him to Sāvatthī, where he taught in the Jeta Garden and made many converts.

The Buddha was once travelling through the cultivated country round Rājagaha at harvest time. All the villagers were out in their fields busily working to reap their crops—none were idle, and even the women came out to help their husbands. Near the village where the Buddha was staying was a large farm belonging to a rich Brahmin. Early one morning the Buddha took his begging-bowl and went to the place where food was being distributed to the labourers. The farmer, seeing the monk waiting for a share of the food, looked displeased, and addressed the Buddha roughly: "I have ploughed my fields," he said, "sown the seed, and gathered in the grain; thus by my toil I have earned my bread. But you, O Gotama, have neither ploughed nor sown; you have done no work to earn your bread."

"I too have ploughed and sown, O Brahmin," replied the Buddha, "and thus I too have earned my bread."

"If this be true," said the Brahmin, "then where is your plough? where are the oxen and the yoke?" Then the Buddha spoke this parable: "The seed I sow is Faith, the rain that waters the seed is Repentance, Wisdom is my plough and yoke, the ox that draws the plough is Diligence; with Truth I cut away the weeds of sin and ignorance; my harvest is the Fruit of Immortality."

When the Buddha first visited his home after his Enlightenment, his son, Rāhula, then quite a young child, was received into the Brotherhood to be trained as a monk. We do not hear much about Rāhula until, at the age of twenty, he was fully ordained in the Jeta Monastery. On this occasion the Buddha addressed his son in a discourse which is still known by the name of the Rāhula sermon.

The Buddha's life had been one of toil and hardship, and, when he was about fifty years old and his strength beginning to fail, the disciples wished to appoint one of their number as his constant companion. The choice fell on Gotama's cousin, Ānanda. Long before, when Ānanda was a boy, a wise man prophesied that he would be the Buddha's attendant. Ānanda's father, not wishing his son to become a monk, did all he could to keep the cousins apart; but, as we heard in an earlier chapter, it was no use, and Ānanda was converted and entered the Order. Ever since that time he had been the Buddha's intimate friend, and now that he was appointed his special attendant, he waited on him with the tenderest care, and never left him till the hour of his death. It was Ānanda's place to carry the Buddha's alms-bowl for him, to spread his mat in the shade of a tree when he was weary and wanted rest, to bring him water when he was thirsty. Ānanda, who was of a gentle and lovable nature, was dearly loved by his Master, and there are many conversations recorded between the two. Neither so great nor intellectual as some of the Buddha's other disciples, Ānanda is the more attractive because of his very human qualities. His devotion knew no limits, and more than once he stood by the Buddha in moments of danger when all the other disciples forsook him.

Can we wonder at the devotion which the Buddha inspired in the hearts of all who knew him! For his love and compassion extended to all mankind, and more than this, to every living being. Of his kindness to animals many instances are recorded. We are apt to pride ourselves on our societies for the protection of animals from the cruelty of man, regarding our humanity as the outcome of our superior civilization. Yet it was more than 2400 years ago that the Buddha said: "In whom there is no compassion for living beings, let one know him as an outcast"; that he urged on his followers the duty of being kind to all creatures, "both those that are strong, and those that tremble in the world"—the weak and helpless. No creature—not the worm lying by the wayside—was too mean for the Buddha's care and tenderness. All living beings, whether men or animals, are of one brotherhood. So taught the Buddha. Was ever a wider charity preached to mankind?

Gotama was once travelling in the land of Magadha when he came on a deer struggling in a snare. He released the poor animal from the meshes that entangled him and let him go free. Then, seating himself at the foot of a tree, Gotama became so deeply wrapped in thought that he never noticed a man who walked stealthily toward him, bow in hand. The enraged hunter, determined to be revenged on the man who had deprived him of his prey, advanced on Gotama with the intention of killing him. Taking aim, he tried to bend his bow, but some power seemed to forbid. His resolution failed him, and he presently laid his bow aside and came to the place where the Buddha was seated.

Few could come into the presence of the Great Teacher without feeling the influence of his noble nature; it was not long before the hunter's anger was softened, and he was listening patiently to the Buddha's words. Presently he went to fetch his wife and children that they too might hear the words of wisdom. In the end the hunter and all the members of his family were converted, professing themselves believers in the doctrine of the Buddha.

Sacrifices were frequently offered by the Brahmins, or Hindu priests, for they believed that it was necessary to appease the gods, and that this could only be done by the shedding of blood. Now there was a certain Brahmin who had made preparations for a great sacrifice in honour of one of the ancient gods of the Hindus. Whole herds of sheep and goats had been collected together, ready to be slaughtered when the day of sacrifice should arrive. It came to pass that the Buddha visited this

Brahmin, and as they sat together, discussing many things, the Buddha spoke of the sacredness of life, whether of men or animals; of the pure heart and upright ways which are of far higher value than a sacrifice necessitating the shedding of blood. For nothing but his own efforts after right-doing can avail a man; he cannot get rid of his sins by making innocent creatures suffer. As the Brahmin listened the Buddha's words sank deep into his soul; he was convinced of their truth and declared himself a believer. Determined to spare the lives of all those animals that had been set apart for the day of sacrifice, the Brahmin ordered that they should be given their freedom. So instead of being slaughtered they were turned loose on the hill-side, where they could roam at will, choose their own pasture, drink the clear water of the mountain streams, and scent the cool breezes that blew on the uplands.

Thus did the Buddha teach his disciples kindness and gentleness toward their fellow creatures, but, more than this, he taught them to love and forgive their enemies, to "overcome anger by not being angered; overcome evil by good; overcome avarice by liberality; overcome falsehoods by truth." He compares the man who is able to curb his anger in the same way that he would control a fiery horse, to "an accomplished driver," while "the vulgar crowd only hold the reins." There are people who pride themselves on a hasty temper, imagining that a display of anger betokens strength of mind. But the Buddha regarded all loss of self-control as a degrading weakness. "There is nothing better than to master one's anger," he says. "The fool that is angered, and who thinks to triumph by using abusive language, is always vanquished by him whose words are patient." We shall hear how Gotama overcame a famous robber by opposing his fury with gentle words.

Journeying in Kosala, the Buddha was warned not to pass through a certain forest, for here, in the deep recesses of the jungle, was the den of a famous robber chief. Angulimāla, as this robber was called, was the terror of the whole country-side, for he lived by plundering unwary travellers, and had committed many murders. He feared no one, and from the very palace of the King the cries of his victims had been heard. All attempts to capture this desperate man had failed, for it was impossible to track him in the dense jungles to which he retired. So he continued his ravages unpunished.

The people of Kosala now besought the Buddha not to expose himself to the dangers of the robber's territory. But Gotama knew no fear, neither man nor beast could affright him; and, heedless of all warnings, he made his way straight to the den of the robber. Angulimāla, enraged at this boldness, determined to slay the intruder. But when he saw the Buddha, calm and self-possessed, and heard his words of kindness, the robber hesitated; his arm, lifted to kill, hung helpless by his side, and his wrath cooled like the embers of a dying fire. As the Buddha reasoned with him he changed his purpose, and, before long, had confessed his sins and declared his faith in the Doctrine. When the people saw the new disciple following his Master they were amazed, and could scarcely believe that this was the same man who had been the terror of their land for so many years. Angulimāla became a monk and was renowned for his holiness. He died not very long after his conversion.

Though many were thus gained over by the

**Gotama and the Robber Chief**

Sidney Stanley

Buddha's kindness and words of wisdom, there were some, even among his own kindred, who were bitterly opposed to Gotama. Yasodharā's father never forgave him for deserting his daughter. That Yasodharā, who might have been a queen, should live a life of poverty, clad in the yellow robes of a nun, her father could not bear to think of; and once, when the Buddha visited his native town, the old Raja went out to meet him, and cursed him before all the people.

But the Buddha's worst enemy was Devadatta. In the days when they were boys together Devadatta had harboured feelings of envy and dislike toward his cousin Siddhattha. You may remember their early quarrel about the wounded goose, whose life Siddhattha saved. As time passed Devadatta's dislike grew into hatred, his ambitious nature could not bear to see another put before himself, and he lost no opportunity of trying to harm Gotama. He even tried to shake Ānanda's loyalty to his Master, but Ānanda refused to listen to him. Though a convert and a member of the Order, Devadatta did all he could to stir up strife among the brethren, and he so far succeeded that about five hundred monks left Gotama and attached themselves to Devadatta.

Being on friendly terms with the son of King Bimbisāra, Devadatta settled himself, with his disciples, at Rājagaha. Devadatta, who practised magic, persuaded the young Prince that he could work miracles and do all kinds of wonderful things, and in this way gained great influence over him. In the end he persuaded the Prince to build him a monastery, and supply his monks with food. Every day the Prince sent chariots bearing five hundred bowls of the choicest kinds of food for these disloyal monks. All this time Devadatta was plotting in his heart how he might supplant the Buddha and become head of the Church. "Gotama is getting old," he said; "it wearies him to do so much preaching, and to direct the affairs of the Brotherhood. Why should he not let me have the management? He could then rest from his labours and live in comfort." Still professing himself a follower of the Buddha, Devadatta asked permission to found a new order of monks, and on being refused, he made up his mind to give up Buddhism and start a new religion of his own. He did not, however, live long enough to carry out his plan. A legend tells that the earth opened and swallowed up Devadatta as a punishment for his wickedness. Of the results of his friendship with Ajātasattu, the son of King Bimbisāra, we shall hear in the next chapter.

# CHAPTER XIII: *The Night of the White Lily*

BIMBISĀRA, King of Magadha, was one of the earliest converts to the Buddhist Faith, and he continued, to the end of his life, to love and reverence the Buddha. This king had a son who was called Ajātasattu, or the Enemy. Why was it that such a name was given to the King's son? I will tell you how it came about.

North of the Ganges, not far from the present town of Patna, once stood the celebrated city of Vesāli. So beautiful was this city, with its fine temples and palaces, its gardens and shady groves, that it seemed an earthly paradise. Its roofs of gold and silver glittered in the sun, and the streets were often gaily decorated to celebrate the many festivals that took place within its walls. Vesāli was divided into three separate districts; in the first there were seven thousand houses with golden towers; in the second, fourteen thousand houses with silver towers; and in the third, twenty-one thousand houses with copper towers. In these three districts the upper, middle, and lower classes of the people lived, according to their rank. Vesāli was not governed by a king; it was known as a Free City, and, like several of the small Indian states in early times, was a kind of republic, the chief magistrate being elected by the people.

Now there was once a chief magistrate of Vesāli who had two daughters. A wise man, who was called in to foretell their future, prophesied that, while the younger one would have a brave and virtuous son, Vassavī, the elder of the two sisters, would give birth to a son who would slay his father and usurp his throne. Vassavī grew up a beautiful maiden, and was as amiable as she was beautiful. Now it happened that Bimbisāra, King of Magadha, came to Vesāli, and, seeing the lovely Vassavī, he fell in love with her and married her. In due time a son was born to her, and, in remembrance of the prophecy, he was named Ajātasattu, or the Enemy.

As the Prince grew up he showed himself of a wayward and unamiable disposition. He was unwise in his choice of companions, and we have already seen how he fell under the influence of Devadatta. The King was much troubled by his son's intimate friendship for such a wicked man, who was an enemy of the Buddha, but Ajātasattu refused to listen to his father's warnings.

Now Devadatta put sinful thoughts into the mind of the young Prince, who became ambitious to possess his father's kingdom, and on one occasion actually attempted his life. Bimbisāra was of a most generous nature, and he not only forgave his son, but made over to him a part of his kingdom, thinking that the Prince's character might improve if he had more responsibility and could take an interest in the welfare of the people. But Ajātasattu plundered and oppressed the people under his rule, so that they complained of his ill-treatment to the King. Bimbisāra was greatly grieved at his son's conduct, but thinking that Ajātasattu might do better with a larger domain and more duties to occupy him, he gave up to him the whole of his kingdom, with the exception of the capital, Rājagaha. Ajātasattu, however, was still dissatisfied, and, acting on the advice of Devadatta, demanded that his father should surrender his capital and his treasury. The old King, who was quite broken down with grief, gave up all he had, but at the same time warned his son against the influence of Devadatta, and entreated him to avoid such a bad companion. Ajātasattu, enraged at his words, had the King seized and cast into prison, and there left to die of starvation. It is sad to think of Bimbisāra, who had been a wise ruler and a kind and tender father, thus imprisoned in his own capital. No one was allowed to visit him except the Queen, who for some time came every day with food for her husband. But when this was discovered, Vassavī was forbidden, on pain of death, to carry anything into the prison. She still contrived, however, to bring the King water, which she hid in her hollow ankle rings; she also brought him nourishing powders concealed in her garments, and by these means managed for a time to keep the King alive. After a while these devices were discovered, and the Queen was forbidden to enter the prison any more.

There was a small window in the prison wall looking in the direction of the Vulture's Peak. The Buddha often stayed on this hill with his disciples, and as the King looked through his narrow window he could sometimes see his beloved Teacher. The sight of the Blessed

One filled the King with so great a joy that it helped to keep him alive. But the poor prisoner was not allowed even this last consolation, for when Ajātasattu heard of it he had the window walled up.

Now it happened that the young son of Ajātasattu had a painful gathering on his finger, and he came crying to his father, who took him in his arms and kissed him. Queen Vassavī wept at the sight, for she thought of the days when her son had been an innocent child. "Ah, just so did thy father to thee!" she cried. And she told the Prince how *his* father had once kissed and petted him on a like occasion. Ajātasattu, hearing this, suddenly realized the wickedness of his conduct. In a fit of remorse he sent to the prison to release his father. But it was too late—the King was dead. Thus was fulfilled the prophecy that Vassavī's son would take the kingdom from his father and slay him.

So Ajātasattu was crowned king of Magadha, and lived in great splendour in his palace at Rājagaha. Although he had been seized with remorse for his conduct toward his father, he still kept up his friendship for Devadatta, and often listened to his advice. The disloyal monk frequently plotted against the Buddha, and when the latter came to Rājagaha, Devadatta made several attempts on his life. There was a man from southern India who was skilled in mechanical arts, and Devadatta directed him to make a kind of catapult from which great rocks could be hurled. This machine was set up above Gotama's dwelling, and some men were hired to work it, and promised great rewards if they should succeed in stoning the Buddha to death. So they lay in wait, watching their opportunity. But when it came to the point these hired murderers refused to act. Overcome by remorse they went to the Buddha, and, kneeling before him, confessed their evil intentions. Before long they were converted.

When Devadatta discovered what had happened, he determined to do the deed himself, and he hurled a large rock, which struck the Buddha on the foot, inflicting a dangerous wound. The disciples, dismayed at seeing their Master wounded, and fearing he might bleed to death, ran to fetch Jīvaka, the physician, who was a half-brother of King Ajātasattu. Jīvaka dressed the Buddha's foot with a very rare ointment made of sandal wood, but it was a long time before he succeeded in healing the wound.

Devadatta, still determined to carry out his wicked purpose, now devised a new plot to bring about Gotama's death. In the King's stables was a very savage elephant; so many people had been attacked and injured by the ferocious beast that at last a petition was sent to the King to beg that a warning bell might be rung whenever the elephant was going to be led out into the streets. This was agreed to, and when the people heard the bell they ran for refuge to the nearest shelter. One day Devadatta, knowing that the Buddha had been invited to the house of a merchant in Rājagaha, went to the elephant-keeper, and promised him a necklace worth a hundred thousand pieces of money if he would let the elephant loose when the Buddha was near. Devadatta, pretending that he had the King's authority for this wicked plot, persuaded the elephant-keeper to carry out his scheme. The Buddha, though he had been warned of his danger, went fearlessly into the city, and was walking up the street, accompanied by many of his disciples, when the warning bell was rung and the elephant let loose. He charged in head-

**The Buddha and the savage Elephant**
Gilbert James

long fury at the crowd of people, and all the disciples fled, terrified, except Ānanda, who remained close to his Master. But Gotama spoke soothing words to the savage beast, who stood still at the sound of his voice, and, becoming completely tamed, followed the Buddha like a dog to the house where he was going. We hear of other instances in which the goodness and holiness of the Buddha gave him power to subdue even the wild beasts. The taming of the elephant is the scene of several carvings on the old Indian monuments.

Not long after these events many of the disloyal monks who had followed Devadatta, repented, and, confessing their sin, returned to the Buddha, who received them back into the Order without a word of reproach. Perhaps King Ajātasattu was beginning to distrust his friend Devadatta, for we hear of his paying a visit to the Buddha, who was staying in a mango grove belonging to Jīvaka the physician.

It was the night of the October full moon—the sacred Night of the White Water-lily.[1] The moon had risen full as the sun, and swam in the heavens like a ball of liquid fire, and the earth, filled with brightness, seemed as though

[1] Translated in Rhys Davids' *Dialogues of the Buddha*, i. 65 f.

strewn with jewels of Paradise. Ajātasattu, moved by the beauty of that October night, went out with all his ministers and stood on the terrace of the palace, in the radiance of the moon. "How beautiful is this night!" exclaimed the King, "how lovely and how peaceful is this moonlight night! In what way can we celebrate it?" "Sire," said one, "you have all that heart can wish, let us deck the city with flowers, and make a festival, and let your Majesty be glad and rejoice." Another suggested a raid on one of the neighbouring tribes, that the night might be celebrated by a victory. And some of the other ministers proposed paying a visit to one or other of the holy men who happened to be staying near. But the King remained silent. Then he turned to Jīvaka the physician. "You have said nothing, Jīvaka," he said. "Sire," replied Jīvaka, "the Buddha is staying in my mango grove, he is above all men in goodness and wisdom, a teacher and guide to mankind. Let your Majesty go to see him, and it may be that he will bring peace to your heart."

Perhaps it was the beauty of that moonlit night that softened the heart of the King and inclined him toward the Buddha, for he said: " Go, Jīvaka, bid them get ready the elephants, and we will visit the Blessed One." Then the great state elephant, a mighty tusker, adorned with trappings covered with gold and precious stones, was brought before the palace. Attendants carrying blazing torches surrounded the King, and in front of him rode the five hundred ladies of the court, each mounted on an elephant. In the silver radiance of that Eastern night the royal procession set forth and came to the mango grove of Jīvaka the physician. No sound was heard from the great company of disciples who were with the Buddha, and for a moment Ajātasattu feared that he had been led into an ambush. Full of anxiety he turned to Jīvaka. " You are not deceiving me," he asked, " and betraying me to my enemies? How is it that from so great an assembly there is no noise, not even the sound of a cough or a sneeze?" " Have no fear, O King," Jīvaka replied, " I am not deceiving you; see, the lamp is burning in the great hall." Then the King alighted from his elephant and entered the monastery on foot; seeing a great multitude of people, he could not, at first, distinguish the Buddha, and asked Jīvaka to point him out. "The Blessed One, O King, is leaning against the middle pillar, with his face toward the East—sitting among his disciples as in the middle of a calm and placid lake." And indeed the King must have felt the spell of that quiet scene, for he exclaimed: "Would that my son might enjoy such peace as now breathes over this assembly!"

Then Ajātasattu bowed himself reverently before the Buddha, and begged permission to question him on various matters about which his mind was in doubt. "Ask, O King, any questions you like," said the Blessed One.

"There are," proceeded the King, "many professions which men follow, such as those of elephant-tamers, horsemen, archers, swordsmen, chariot-drivers, weavers, cooks, washermen, basket-makers, barbers, clerks, and many others. The men following all these professions have their reward, for they make a living and are able to enjoy comfort and support their parents and children. Now is there, in this world, any reward for the man who becomes a monk—who renounces home and kindred, wealth, and all the comforts and pleasures of life?" The King said that he had put the same question to several Brahmins and Hindu philosophers, but none of them had been able to give him a satisfactory answer.

" I will ask you a question," said the Buddha. " Suppose that one of your servants should renounce the world, shave his hair and beard, put on the yellow robes, and live in solitude, content with the bare necessaries of life—how would you treat that man? would you force him to return to his duties?" "Nay," answered the King, " we should treat him with reverence, rise from our seat in his presence and bid him be seated, prepare him a dwelling-place, provide him with food, robes, and medicines, and all that he might require."

" Then," said the Buddha, " have you not shown that there is, in this world, a reward for him who leads the higher life?" The King agreed. " This is but the first reward," the Buddha explained, and he went on to show that there are other and higher rewards for him who casts off the burden of earthly passions and earthly ties. Free as the air is his life who has ceased to care for wealth and all those things over which men worry and fret themselves. Unburdened by possessions, like a bird on the wing he can go whithersoever it pleases him, wanting nothing but just sufficient food to support life, and clothing to cover him. His resting-place is in some quiet spot—a breezy hill-side, a shady grove, or mountain glen. Thus the monk learns contentment. Having trained himself in virtue, he lives at peace with all men, full of kindness and compassion toward every living creature. Like a king who has overcome all his enemies, has he subdued his passions, banishing worry and fretfulness, hatred, ill-nature and indolence. With a mind intent on the things which alone are worth possessing, he becomes serene and calm. And happiness arising within him fills his whole being, as the springs of the earth may fill a deep pool with clear cool water, though no stream flows into it, and no rains fall."

Thus did the Buddha convince King Ajātasattu that there is a reward, even in this world, for him who renounces all to lead the higher life. The King's heart was touched as he pondered over the Buddha's words. "Excellently has the Blessed One spoken!" he exclaimed, "as a man who brings a lamp into the darkness that the things which are hidden may become visible; even so hast thou shown me the Truth, O Blessed One! Henceforth will I put my trust in the Buddha, the Doctrine, and the Brotherhood. I have fallen into sin, O my Lord, for I sinned grievously in putting to death my father, that good and just man. May the Blessed One accept my confession!"

"Truly you have sinned, O King," replied the Buddha, "but, because you have recognized your sin, and acknowledged it, we accept your confession. For he who rightly sees and confesses his sin will in time learn self-control."

The night was far advanced and the moon sinking toward the horizon when the King took his leave and departed. When he was gone the Buddha spoke to the disciples. The King, he told them, had been deeply moved, and if he had not borne a heavy sin on his conscience would have been converted. But the eye of the soul when blinded by sin is unable to behold the Truth.

# CHAPTER XIV: *The Buddha's Last Journey*

MANY years had passed since the Buddha began his ministry. He was now old and infirm, but he still travelled from village to village, teaching the people and sympathizing with their sorrows. When the rainy season came on he retired to one or other of the garden monasteries, where the disciples would gather round their Master for counsel and instruction. One of Gotama's favourite resorts was the Jeta Garden near Sāvatthi, and here he passed the forty-fourth Lent since his Enlightenment. This was the last season which the Buddha spent in that pleasant retreat. From Sāvatthi he travelled to Rājagaha, a long and weary journey, and took up his abode on the hill called the Vulture's Peak.

[1] Now King Ajātasattu was about to declare war on the Vajjians, the tribes inhabiting the country north of the Ganges, where the famous city of Vesāli stood. Doubtful as to his chances of success, the King determined to consult the Buddha, so he sent his Prime

[1] Translated in Rhys Davids' *Dialogues of the Buddha*, ii. 78 f.

Minister to the Vulture's Peak. When the Prime Minister had saluted the Buddha and made inquiries after his health, he delivered the King's message. The King, he said, had resolved to attack the Vajjians; would he overcome his enemies and destroy them utterly? The Buddha replied that so long as the Vajjians remained united among themselves, true to their established customs and the precepts he had once laid down for them—so long as they honoured their elders and holy men, and paid respect to their shrines, an invader would have no power to overcome them.

When the Prime Minister had taken his departure the Buddha summoned all the brethren and spoke to them of the importance of unity and right conduct. So long, he said, as the brethren continued to assemble together in perfect concord, respected their elders and obeyed the rules of the Order, adding nothing nor taking away anything of that already laid down; so long as they walked in the paths of righteousness, keeping themselves free from worldly concerns, and avoiding idle talk and gossip, the religion of the Buddha would not decline but prosper.

When Gotama had stayed some time on the

Vulture's Peak, he left Rājagaha with a large company of disciples and travelled northward, visiting many villages on his way. Coming to the river Ganges, he crossed it at a point where King Ajātasattu was building a strong fortress as a defence against the Vajjians. In years to come a great city was to occupy this site—Pātaliputta, the new capital of Magadha. At the present day the city of Patna stands near the spot where the Buddha crossed the Ganges for the last time.

Having visited Vesāli the Buddha spent the following rainy season in a village near-by. Here he was attacked by sickness, and for some time suffered great pain and weakness, but he bore these ills without complaint. Ānanda, who tended him, was overcome with grief, fearing that his Master would die. One day, when he was getting better, and was sitting on a folded mat outside the monastery, Ānanda came and sat near his Master, and told him of the misery he had gone through when he feared he might lose him. " Thy Master," said the Buddha, " has reached four-score years, his body is bent and infirm, and just as an old, worn-out cart, which is bound up with cords, can with difficulty be kept going, so is it only with care and trouble that this body continues to exist. I am old, Ānanda, my journey is nearly ended, but sorrow not, and let the Truth be your refuge."

The Buddha, knowing that his life must soon draw to a close, told Ānanda to summon all the disciples who were in the neighbourhood of Vesāli. When they had met together he earnestly enjoined them to spread the truths of pure religion for the good and happiness of mankind. When the rainy season was over, the Buddha set forth to visit the villages round about, and as he left Vesāli he turned and gazed long at the city, for he knew that he looked on it for the last time. Passing from village to village in a north-westerly direction, the Buddha came to a place called Pāvā, where he stayed in a mango grove belonging to Chunda, a worker of metals. When Chunda heard that the Blessed One was staying in his mango grove he invited him and all his disciples to come to his house on the following day. In the early morning Chunda made all ready for the feast, and provided sweet cakes and rice and mushrooms. Then he went to the mango grove to bid his guests come, for the meal was ready. It was the custom in Eastern lands for the householder to collect his guests when the feast was prepared. We read in the Bible of the king who "sent forth his servants to call them that were bidden to the marriage feast." As Buddhist monks eat only one meal a day, which must be taken between sunrise and noon, those wishing to show them hospitality invite them to a morning meal. The Buddha, having robed himself, took his bowl and went with his disciples to the house of Chunda the metal worker. When all had been served, Chunda took a seat at the Master's feet to listen to his words.

Now that same day Gotama was attacked by sickness; toward evening, however, he was able to start on his way to Kusinārā, a small town lying south of Pāvā. But his footsteps were weary, and he was often obliged to rest by the way, for the end of life's journey was nearly reached. Once, when he was resting under a tree near a stream, he asked Ānanda to fetch him some water, for he was thirsty. But Ānanda, knowing that a caravan of five hundred bullock carts had just crossed the ford above, feared the water would be foul and muddy. The Buddha repeated his request a second, and again a third time, so Ānanda went down to the brook. To his surprise the water was clear as crystal. "How great is the power of the Master!" he exclaimed, thinking that a miracle had been performed. He filled a bowl with clear cool water and carried it to the Buddha, who drank and was much revived. The next halt was made on the banks of a beautiful river, and the Buddha and his disciples went down to the water to bathe. During the heat of the day they rested in a mango grove on the farther shore.

Thus by slow and painful stages the Buddha continued his journey until he came to Kusinārā, a little mud-built town in the midst of the jungle. Near-by was a grove of sala-trees, and here Ānanda prepared a couch for his Master. Between two twin sala-trees—so called because they were of exactly equal size—the Buddha laid him down to rest, with his head to the north. All at once the two sala-trees beneath which he lay burst into bloom, and the blossoms fell in a shower over his body, while sounds of heavenly music floated in the sky in honour of the Blessed One.

As the Buddha lay in the sala grove, calm and self-possessed, he spoke long with Ānanda about the Order and the rules to be observed by the brethren when he should no longer be there to guide them. At the close of the discourse Ānanda was overcome with sorrow. He saw that his Master was dying, and he went away by himself and shed bitter tears, so unbearable was the thought that his beloved Master was about to leave him. The Buddha noticed Ānanda's absence. " Where is Ānanda ? " he asked, and he sent one of the brethren to call him. " Do not grieve, Ānanda," said the Buddha, when his disciple was seated near him, " it must always be thus, the time of parting with those we love *must* come, sooner or later ; for it is in the nature of everything that is born into the world that it must also die. How could it be otherwise ? For a long time you have been very near me, Ānanda ; by many acts of kindness and a love which has never varied you have done well. Cease not to strive, and you too shall before long attain the Peace of Nirvana." Then the Buddha spoke to the assembled brethren of his cousin's kindness and thoughtfulness and his many good qualities. Presently he sent Ānanda into the town to tell the people of Kusinārā that the Buddha lay, near to death, in the grove of sala-trees. The nobles of Kusinārā were assembled in the council hall, and Ānanda went in and told them that before morning dawned the Blessed One would pass away. When the people heard the news they could not contain their grief—many flung themselves weeping on the ground, the women dishevelled their hair, uttering loud lamentations, and all gave way to their sorrow, overcome with the thought that the Light of the World would vanish away. And during the first watch of the night the men of Kusinārā, each with his family and his household, came to visit the dying Buddha, to do him reverence.

There was a young Brahmin philosopher called Subhadda, staying in Kusinārā. Having doubts concerning his faith, he greatly desired to speak with the Buddha, and came for this purpose to the sala grove. But Ānanda refused to disturb his Master. "Trouble him not," he said, "he is weary." Gotama, hearing voices, asked who was there, and had the Brahmin admitted. So Subhadda came into the Buddha's presence, and, having courteously saluted him, questioned him on the doctrines of the great Hindu philosophers, asking which of these understood the Truth. But the great

Teacher bid him let be these learned discussions; true religion must teach, before all else, the practice of virtue; only in the earnest endeavour after right-doing, in the steps of the Noble Eightfold Path, can Peace be found. As Subhadda listened to the Buddha's words, all doubt left his mind, and he was converted. "Like one," he said, "who shows the path to him who has gone astray, or brings a lamp to lighten our darkness, even so hast thou shown me the Truth, O Blessed One!" The young Brahmin begged to be accepted as a disciple, and Ānanda, taking him aside, received him into the Order. He poured water on his head, shaved his hair and beard, and put the yellow robes on him. Then Subhadda repeated the 'Three Refuges': "I go for refuge to the Buddha, I go for refuge to the Truth, I go for refuge to the Brotherhood"; and returning to his Master, took his seat beside him. Subhadda was the last man whom the Buddha converted.

When the Buddha had again spoken with Ānanda, he asked whether, of all the disciples present, there were any who had doubts about his teaching, inviting those who might wish to make inquiries to speak freely. But all

**The Passing of the Buddha**
Sidney Stanley

the brethren were silent. The Buddha put the same question a second, and again a third time, but there was not one of all those present who had any doubt or misgiving.

The night wore on as the disciples watched beside their dying Master in the quiet sala grove. And in the third watch of the night the Buddha passed away.

. . . . . .

With solemn ceremony, and such honours as they would have bestowed on the body of the greatest king, did the people of Kusinārā reverence the remains of the Blessed One. The nobles, followed by all the people, walked in procession to the sala grove, bearing garlands of flowers, perfumes and sweet spices, harps and flutes and other musical instruments. Over the place where the Buddha lay they made a canopy on which were hung wreaths of lotus flowers, and until the close of day the people honoured the remains with hymns and music and religious rites.

When all was ready for the burning of the body, eight chieftains of Kusinārā carried the Blessed One through the midst of the city, entering by the northern gate and passing out through the eastern gate to the place where the funeral pile had been prepared. The procession moved slowly, for the narrow streets were crowded with people, who strewed the way with flowers and sweetly scented spices. When the body had been consumed by fire and all the ceremonies duly performed, the ashes were placed in the council hall. To guard the sacred spot the warriors of Kusinārā made a rampart with their bows, and planted their spears crosswise, like a lattice work. And without the council hall was a line of elephants, another of horsemen, and another of chariots. For seven days the people paid honours to the relics with garlands of flowers, with music, and solemn dances.

When it became known that the Buddha had died in Kusinārā, Ajātasattu, King of Magadha, sent to beg for a portion of the ashes, for he wished to build a cairn or monument over them and hold a yearly festival in the Buddha's honour. The people of Vesāli made the same request.

Likewise the Sakyas of Kapilavatthu.

In all the lands where the Buddha had been known and loved, the people wished to honour him and keep his memory fresh in their minds. There were, in all, eight messengers who came to Kusinārā to beg for a share of the ashes. At first the nobles of Kusinārā refused to part with the relics, for the Blessed One had died in their land, and they considered that his remains should rest there. A heated discussion might have arisen had not a Brahmin, who was a believer, addressed the people and pointed out how wrong it would be if strife should arise over the remains of the greatest of mankind, who had always taught peace and forbearance. In the end the relics were divided into eight portions, and over these were built eight cairns, in different parts of the country. These monuments were usually in the form of a solid dome, in which there was a small treasure chamber to contain the relics. The ruins of some of the ancient cairns have been discovered and excavated; they must have been of immense size, as, for instance, that built by the Buddha's own countrymen, the Sakyas, which is said to have been as large as the dome of St Paul's Cathedral.

Such monuments are seen in all Buddhist countries—in Ceylon they are called Dāgabas, in other places Topes, or Stupas. They are raised to keep alive the memory of holy men, and do not necessarily contain relics. The people bring offerings of flowers to these shrines, staying a while to meditate, and, "at the thought, 'This is the Dāgaba of that Blessed One, the Buddha,' the hearts of many are made calm and happy."

# CHAPTER XV: *The Spread of the Faith*

WE have seen how the great reformer, Gotama the Buddha, purified the religious beliefs of his native land, and put before his countrymen a higher ideal than was ever realized by mankind before the age of Christianity. To look upon the whole world—upon every living being in it—with feelings of love and sympathy, to overcome even hatred with love, to follow virtue for its own sake, looking for no reward beyond the inward peace and tranquillity of the heart—*this* is what the Buddha expected of his followers. It seems a great deal to expect of human nature; yet this religion which demands so much, and appears to promise so little, has attracted many followers. For Buddhism prevails over a large part of the continent of Asia—in Ceylon, Burma, Siam, Japan, China, Tibet, and other places, there are five hundred millions of men and women who profess the faith of the Buddha. So far have its conquests extended; yet Buddhism is perhaps the only religion which has never made use of the sword as a means of spreading its doctrines.

When a religion is professed by widely different races of mankind—differing in their ideas and ways of thinking—it is impossible that its practice should be exactly the same in the various countries in which it has taken root. And, as the Christianity of Rome differs from that of a sect like the Quakers, so does the Buddhism of Tibet, with its elaborate rites and ceremonies, differ from the simpler form of the Faith, as practised in Ceylon and Burma. You may think, perhaps, that Buddhism still flourishes in India, the land of its birth, but this is not so. Although the Faith grew and spread on Indian soil during several centuries, in the end Brahminism regained its influence over the people, and at the present time the Buddha's doctrines are almost unknown in the land where he lived and taught for so many years. But though the Buddhist religion is no longer professed by the people of India, its influence is not dead. The Buddha's teaching still survives in principles of love and kindness toward all creatures and in many of the charitable societies of modern Hinduism.

After the Buddha's death, which took place in the year 480 B.C., the small Indian states, of which we have heard in our story, passed through various changes. In the course of many wars and disturbances the Kingdom of Magadha gradually enlarged its boundaries, annexing most of the surrounding states. The capital of Magadha, formerly Rājagaha, was now Pātaliputta, a great and splendid city, standing on the site of the present town of Patna. The ruins of Pātaliputta have been traced, but, as they lie buried at a depth of nearly twenty feet below the modern town, they are difficult to excavate. Magadha took a leading place among the Indian states, and at the time of the invasion of India by Alexander the Great, in 327 B.C., it was a large and powerful kingdom.

On the death of Alexander his great empire was split up into separate kingdoms, of which there were several in the north-west of India. But within a year of Alexander's death the people in these conquered provinces revolted. Their leader was a young man named Chandagutta, who was related to the royal family of Magadha. He had once been a robber chief, and must have had great abilities, for he succeeded in freeing his countrymen and driving the Greek invaders out of India. When a revolution broke out at Pātaliputta, Chandagutta headed the rebels, who proved victorious; the King was dethroned and put to death with all the members of his family, and Chandagutta was proclaimed king of Magadha. He reigned for twenty-four years, and was a capable, though in some ways a harsh, ruler. Chandagutta greatly enlarged his dominions by conquest, and, having for the first time in history brought the greater part of the Indian peninsula under the same rule, he may be called the first Emperor of India. He was succeeded by his son, Bindusāra, who reigned for twenty-eight years, but of whom very little is known.

The great Indian Empire, founded by Chandagutta, was now inherited by his grandson, Asoḳa, who ascended the throne in the year 273 B.C. Like his father and grandfather, Asoka was brought up in the faith of the Brahmins. He proved himself a wise and just ruler, and during his reign of forty years did much for the welfare of his vast dominions.

In the thirteenth year of his reign Asoka made war on Kalinga, a kingdom bordering upon the Bay of Bengal. There was a great deal of fighting and bloodshed before Kalinga was subdued. Those slain in battle numbered a hundred thousand, while many more were carried away captive or died of disease. In the end Asoka's army was victorious, and Kalinga became a province of the Indian Empire.

When we read the lives of the great conquerors whose names have become famous in history—Alexander, Napoleon, and others—we see how success increased their thirst for conquest. Regardless of the misery that follows the track of an invading army, they continued to plan fresh campaigns, always longing for more lands to subdue.

Far other was the effect of conquest on the Indian King. Asoka was stricken to the heart by the thought of the misery he had caused in Kalinga, and the results of his remorse were far-reaching. How is it that we know so much of the thoughts of this Indian King, who lived more than two thousand years ago? When Asoka issued his edicts, or proclamations, he ordered them to be cut on rocks and stone pillars. Throughout the length and breadth of India these ancient monuments are found, engraved with the words of the great Emperor Asoka.

Some of the inscriptions are on tall, graceful

pillars, often beautifully decorated with carvings of flowers and animals; some are cut on rocks and caves, in wild, deserted spots, overspread by a tangled network of jungle. For a long time no one understood these records, for they are written in a forgotten language. By degrees, however, after careful and patient study, scholars learnt to read them. Thus it comes about that, at the present day, the actual words of Asoka can be traced and their meaning understood. How strange it seems that these rock-cut letters should be able to tell us the thoughts that were in the King's mind so many centuries ago!

One of the most interesting of the edicts was published four years after the conquest of Kalinga, and we learn of the "deep sorrow and regret" felt by "His Sacred Majesty" for the misery he had caused by the war. In the words of the King, "One hundred and fifty thousand persons were carried away captive, one hundred thousand were slain, and many times that number perished." Asoka goes on to tell us of the remorse he felt for having conquered Kalinga, "because the conquest of a country previously unconquered involves the slaughter, death, and carrying away captive of the people." He regrets that there should be holy men and other innocent persons who, as a result of the war, have suffered misfortune and hardship. But the most important announcement of this edict is that " Directly after the annexation of Kalinga, began His Sacred Majesty's zealous protection of the Law of Piety, his love of that Law, and his giving instruction in that Law." The 'Law of Piety' to which the King refers is the Doctrine of the Buddha. This, then, was the result of Asoka's remorse—he adopted the Faith which seeks, not to kill, but to spare life, which aims at bringing happiness to all living creatures. His sorrow for having been the cause of suffering to innocent people was not an empty, passing regret, for, from the day that he embraced the Faith of the Buddha, Asoka did all in his power to promote the happiness and welfare of his people. " All men are my children," says Asoka, " and just as I desire for my children that they may enjoy every kind of prosperity and happiness in both this world and the next, so also I desire the same for all men." In speaking of the unsubdued tribes on the borders of the empire, Asoka desires that they should not be afraid of him, that they should trust him, and should receive from him happiness, not sorrow. Was not this King, who conquered himself, far greater than those rulers who conquered nations and kingdoms, and left behind them the remembrance of untold sorrow and misery?

For two and a half years after his conversion Asoka was a lay disciple; then he entered the Order, and from that time fulfilled the double duties of monk and ruler of a vast empire. He worked hard for the good of his people, and in many ways improved their condition. Roads and bridges were made, wells were dug, and trees planted. Rest-houses were built along all the high roads, and arrangements made for the comfort of travellers. Hospitals, both for men and animals, were established in all parts of the empire. Perhaps you may not know that Buddhists were the first people to build hospitals, and to give special attention to the care of the sick. To this day there are animal hospitals in several places in India—memorials of the Buddhists' kindness to animals.

Asoka did a great deal for the bodily welfare of his people, but the best gift he could make them was, he thought, instruction in the

Buddha's doctrine. So he sent teachers into all parts of the Empire, for Buddhism had not, as yet, spread over the whole of the Indian Peninsula. Laws were made to insure the keeping of the Buddha's precepts, especially with regard to the kind treatment of animals. Beasts were no longer to be slaughtered for sacrifice, and it was forbidden to kill certain kinds of birds and animals which were of no use for food. The Royal Hunt was abolished, and the King, instead of going on hunting expeditions, as he had been used to do before his conversion, made pilgrimages to the sacred places of the Buddhists. Twice he visited the birthplace of the Buddha, where he erected a pillar with the inscription, "Here was the Holy One born." Asoka made pilgrimages to the scenes of the chief events in the Buddha's life—the sacred Bo-tree beneath which Gotama obtained wisdom, the Jeta Monastery where so much of his teaching was given, and the sala grove at Kusinārā, where the Buddha passed away. Many monasteries and stupas were erected by Asoka, and near the sacred Bo-tree he built a beautiful temple whose remains can still be traced.

Though Asoka was so attached to the faith

he had adopted, he always showed a tolerant spirit toward those who professed different beliefs. One of his edicts on the subject of toleration begins thus: "His Sacred and Gracious Majesty does reverence to men of all sects." In accordance with the Buddha's teaching Asoka valued right conduct above forms and ceremonies; that a man should act up to his beliefs was, he thought, the thing of chief importance.

During Asoka's reign a great church council was held at Pātaliputta. At this council the Buddhist Scriptures were recited, and the Doctrine clearly laid down, for there had been heresies and divisions in the Buddhist Church as in all other religious communities. This was the third council held by the elders of the Church since the Buddha's death.

Not content with having established the Faith in his own dominions, Asoka now set forward a scheme for spreading the Buddha's teaching in foreign lands. Think of the vast size of such an undertaking in days when the means of travelling were so different from those of our own time! Missionaries were dispatched to the Himālayan region and the border lands to the north-west of the Empire, with the result that, in time, the Faith penetrated into Tibet, China, Mongolia, Korea, and Japan, in which places it still flourishes. Missions were also sent into Western Asia, Eastern Europe, and even to Northern Africa. To the island of Ceylon, Asoka sent his son (or, as some say, his younger brother) Mahinda, who had joined the Order of Monks twelve years before. Mahinda landed in Ceylon with a band of monks, and was well received by the King, who, before long, became a convert to Buddhism, many of his subjects following his example. The capital of Ceylon was, in those days, Anurādhapura, and there the King built a great monastery and a magnificent dāgaba, which is still to be seen.

Mahinda passed the remainder of his life in Ceylon. Not far from Anurādhapura is a beautiful hill, standing high above the surrounding plains; on the western slope of this hill a little chamber has been hollowed out of the rock; this quiet retreat, far removed from the din of the great city, was Mahinda's study. Here, also, he died, after a long life spent in labouring for the good of others.

You will remember that, when the Buddha first learned the wisdom which enabled him to become a teacher of mankind, he was seated, meditating, under a peepul-tree on the borders of the Uruvela jungle. This tree, since called the Bo-tree, or Tree of Wisdom, was looked upon with great veneration, for was it not beneath its branches that the Buddha entered into the Great Peace! It was natural that the new converts in Ceylon should wish to plant a cutting of the sacred tree, and they sent to King Asoka to beg for a branch. The King's daughter, who had entered the Order, came to Ceylon with a band of nuns, and brought the precious cutting with her. It was planted at Anurādhapura, where it grew and flourished, and there it is still to be seen—the oldest historical tree in the world. The monks who live in one of the old monasteries still carefully tend the tree, now over two thousand years old, which they treasure as a memorial of their beloved Master. There is now little to be seen of the once magnificent city of Anurādhapura, for most of it lies buried beneath a network of jungle.

Though Buddhism may differ in many ways from our own creed, we cannot but reverence a Faith which has been the guiding light of so many of our fellow-men. Like Asoka, let us honour those, of whatever sect, who follow the truth which has been given them.

A man who was seeking the Truth once went to the Buddha and asked him: "Where, in the midst of this troubled river of life, encompassed by death and decay, can I find an island—a refuge from the evil of the world?" There is an island, the Buddha told him, where death has no power—Nirvana, the everlasting Peace. And since those words were spoken many myriads of men and women have steered their course for that 'other shore,' secure in the Buddha's promise that there they shall find Peace!

# BOOKS CONSULTED

*Buddhism.* Rhys Davids.

*Buddhism.* Mrs Rhys Davids.

*The Life of the Buddha.* W. Rockhill.

*The Life of Gaudama.* Bigandet.

*Buddha.* Trans. from the German of Oldenberg.

*Buddhist Birth Stories.* Rhys Davids.

*Buddhist Suttas.* Trans. by Rhys Davids.

*Dialogues of the Buddha.* Trans. by Rhys Davids.

*The Dhammapada and Sutta-Nipâta.* Max Müller and Fausböll.

*Buddhism.* Coplestone.

*Buddhist India.* Rhys Davids.

*Asoka.* (Rulers of India Series.) Vincent Smith.